The Western Photographs
of John K. Hillers

Don D. Fowler

Smithsonian Institution Press
Washington and London

MYSELF IN

The Western Photographs of
JOHN K. HILLERS

THE WATER

Contents

Dedicated to the memory of
Clifford Evans
Friend and Guru

Library of Congress
Cataloging-in-Publication Data
Fowler, Don D.
   The western photographs of
John K. Hillers: "myself in the water"
/ Don D. Fowler.
      p.   cm.
   Bibliography: p.
   ISBN 0-87474-416-4
   ISBN 0-87474-441-5 (pbk.)
   1. Photography—West (U.S.)—
Landscapes.   2. West (U.S.)—Description and
travel— 1860–1880—Views.   3. West (U.S.)—
Description and travel—1880–1950—
Views.   4. Colorado River Valley (Colo.-
Mexico)—Description and travel—
Views.   5. Indians of North America—
Southwest, New—Pictorial works.   6. Hillers,
John K., 1843–1925.
I. Hillers, John K., 1843–1925.   II. Title.
TR660.F68   1989   88–23950
770'.92'4—dc19   CIP
British Library Cataloguing-in-Publication data
is available.

⊗ The paper used in this publication meets the
minimum requirements of the American
National Standard for Permanence of Paper for
Printed Library Materials Z39.48–1984.

Printed in the United States of America
10   9   8   7   6   5   4   3   2   1
98 97 96 95 94 93 92 91 90 89

Southern Paiute Indians and Mormons meet
outside St. George, Utah, in September 1873.

Preface

When Jack Hillers's diary was published in 1972, there was a call for a general retrospective of his career as a photographer. The present volume is a somewhat belated response to that call. It covers Hillers's active years as a photographer, from his first attempts in 1871–72 until his retirement from full-time work in 1900. The record presented here is not as full as one would wish, primarily because Hillers, unlike many other government employees, left but a scant "paper trail." Apparently because of his close friendship with John Wesley Powell, who was Hillers's boss from 1871 to 1894, Hillers worked for the most part under verbal rather than written orders. The files of the Powell Survey, the Bureau of American Ethnology, and the U.S. Geological Survey contain very few documents on, by, or about Hillers. Nonetheless, I hope that I have presented his work clearly and accurately.

This volume also presents, for the first time, a selection of Hillers's photographs taken in Indian Territory (Oklahoma) in 1875. In his diary Hillers listed a series of photographs he took during a trip there to photograph Indians for an exhibit in the Government Building at the 1876 Centennial Exhibition in Philadelphia. When Hillers's diary was being prepared for publication, a number of the photographs mentioned in the diary could not be found. After the diary appeared in print, Gary Kurutz, then with the Huntington Library, San Marino, California, called my attention to a collection of glass plate negatives and photographs that had been quietly resting in the basement of the Library since 1900. They had been donated by George W. Ingalls, who was with Hillers in Indian Territory in 1875 and had been with Powell and Hillers in southern Utah and Nevada in 1873. The Ingalls Collection contains all but one of the "lost" Indian Terri-

John K. (Jack) Hillers, 1843–1925.
Smithsonian Institution.

tory photographs that Hillers recorded taking. (The missing photograph is explained in the third chapter.) My profound gratitude goes to Gary Kurutz for locating the photographs and to the Huntington Library for generous permission to reproduce photographs from the Ingalls Collection.

Numerous others have provided assistance and support. Norma Mikkelsen and Paula Roberts were of great assistance in the early planning stages of the volume. The late Clifford Evans and his spouse and colleague, Betty Meggers, provided warm hospitality and help during my numerous trips to Washington, D.C., on the trail of Hillers and Powell esoterica.

The staff members of the Still Pictures Division of the National Archives and Records Service in Washington, D.C., were most helpful. Herman J. Viola, James Glenn, and Paula Richardson Fleming of the Smithsonian Institution's National Anthropological Archives have been of great help and have sustained a keen interest in the project over a number of years. Wendy T. Wright, an intern in the Anthropological Archives in 1981, went out of her way to be helpful in collecting information on the persons shown in figs. 102–105. Augie Mastrogiuseppe and David Myers of the Western History Collection, Denver Public Library, Mrs. Manon B. Atkins of the Oklahoma Historical Society, Oklahoma City, and Alan Clark Miller of the International Museum of Photography, George Eastman House, Rochester, New York, all were most helpful. Thomas D. Burke and Joseph A. Mobley of the North Carolina Department of Cultural Resources, Raleigh, provided valuable information relating to places Hillers photographed in North Carolina and Georgia.

My mother, Ruby Noyes Tippets, deserves particular and special thanks for many devoted hours spent at the microfilm readers and computer terminals of the Utah Genealogical Society, Salt Lake City, in a somewhat frustrating search for records on Hillers, his ancestors, and his parents. There too, Hillers's paper trail proved thin, but very valuable. Thanks are also due to my colleague Michael Brodhead for advice on details of the organization of the Union army during the Civil War, and the U.S. Army in years following the conflict. Ella Kleiner word-processed earlier drafts of the volume and did bibliographical checking with elan and competence. The maps were drafted by Patti de Bunch.

A particular note of thanks goes to Richard McKenzie, Jack Hillers's great-grandson, who shared with me Hillers's album of his own prints, made for his own enjoyment sometime between 1892 and 1900. The album contains about sixty 11 × 14 inch prints, prints Hillers personally wanted to keep. My warmest thanks to Mr. McKenzie for his hospitality and his interest in this book. I very much appreciate the editorial acumen of Matthew Abbate on the final draft of the book.

Finally, my deepest appreciation, as always, goes to Kay Fowler, whose interest and encouragement make it all worthwhile.

DON D. FOWLER

The Western Photographs
of John K. Hillers

Down the Colorado

A Chance Meeting

Sometime in the second week of May 1871, John K. (Jack) Hillers met Major John Wesley Powell in Salt Lake City, Utah Territory. The meeting was a fateful one, especially for Hillers. It would lead him into a thirty-year career as an acclaimed photographer of American Indians and landscapes, a career he could scarcely have envisioned as a recently discharged U.S. Army sergeant in search of employment as a teamster.

In 1869 Powell had led the first boating expedition through the unknown and uncharted canyons of the Colorado River. Now, Powell and his brother-in-law, Almon Harris Thompson, were in Salt Lake City preparing for a second boat trip. They needed an extra boatman and somehow found Hillers, who decided that such work would be more interesting than trekking overland in charge of recalcitrant mules or plodding oxen. According to Hillers family legend, he had been working as a teamster in San Francisco but was returning east and had only been in Salt Lake City a few hours when he met Powell.

Powell and Hillers struck a deal and at 5:00 A.M. on May 15, 1871, they and Thompson boarded a train for Green River City, Wyoming Territory. Powell's new boatman was twenty-eight years old, just under six feet tall, with blue eyes, reddish-sandy hair, an affable disposition

and often ribald wit, and he liked to sing. Hillers's good nature and easy humor appealed to Powell. In later years, Hillers was one of the very few of Powell's employees or associates whom Powell permitted to joke openly with him.

John K. (originally Johann Karl) Hillers had been born December 20, 1843, in Brinkum, in the then-kingdom of Hannover (English: Hanover), Germany. In 1852 the Hillers family emigrated to the United States, possibly stopping for a time in Hull, England, before continuing on. Like tens of thousands of other emigrants, the family settled in New York City.[1] There Hillers became friends with Irish lads in his neighborhood. Frederick S. Dellenbaugh, the young expedition artist who shared boatman duties with Hillers, later wrote: "As a boy in New York, Jack though not a Hiberion [sic] himself, had closely associated with descendants of the Shamrock Isle, and he could speak with a fine emerald brogue. . . . Jack had many times followed in the wake of the 13 Eagles Fire Company, one of the bright jewels with a green setting, of the old volunteer service. The foreman . . . was Irish too and his stentorian shout through the trumpet [was] 'Tirtaan Aigles, dis wai.' . . . The Aigles were in for glory, nothing else. So when we [during the river trip] heard the roar of a rapid and sniffed the mist in the air, 'Tirtaan Aigles, dis wai,' was our slogan."[2]

It is not known how much formal schooling young Jack Hillers acquired. He was apparently working as a clerk in New York City when the Civil War began. He may have enlisted initially in the New York Naval Brigade (despite its name a coastal artillery unit). But War Department records and Hillers's pension records indicate that he was formally enlisted in the regular U.S. Army on

1. Start of the 1871 river trip, Green River, Wyoming, May 17 or 18, 1871. Left to right: *Canonita*, E. O. Beaman, A. J. Hattan, W. C. Powell; *Emma Dean*, S. V. Jones, J. K. Hillers, J. W. Powell, F. S. Dellenbaugh; *Nellie Powell*, A. H. Thompson, J. F. Steward, F. M. Bishop. E. O. Beaman photograph. U.S. Geological Survey Photo Library, Denver, Colorado.

June 13, 1861, at Fort Monroe, Virginia, where he was assigned as a private in L Company of the Fourth Artillery Regiment, commanded by Captain Robert V. W. Howard. The regiment was a unit of the Army of the James.[3]

The muster rolls for L Company report Hillers "Present, sick in hospital, Ft. Monroe," on October 31, 1861. On June 30, 1862, he was reported "present for duty" at a camp near Suffolk, Virginia. There, in either June or July 1862 Hillers "sustained a severe injury to his back by reason of lifting a piece of light artillery in manoeuvering." Because there was no unit doctor, he was not treated but sent to his tent and later "placed in charge of the Captain's horse." The injury plagued him periodically for the rest of his life.[4]

It is not clear how much action Hillers's unit saw between 1861 and 1864. The principal role of the Army of the James was static—to control and hold the entrance to the James River and Chesapeake Bay. Hillers's unit may have participated in some skirmishes in and around Suffolk, Virginia, in 1862, but it was apparently not involved in General George C. McClellan's Peninsular Campaign of that year. The paucity of information in Hillers's army records suggests that he spent most of his time with his unit in reserve. Hillers reenlisted in February 1864. The L Company muster roll for February 29, 1864, reports that he was discharged on February 1, 1864, at Yorktown, Virginia, and reenlisted the next day in the same outfit, still a private.[5]

As the Union forces began to close in on Richmond, Virginia, the Confederate capital, in 1864, Hillers finally did see some action. In May 1864 a portion of the Army of the James, the Eighteenth Army Corps under the command of Major General William F. Smith, was temporarily attached to the Army of the Potomac. The detachment included Hillers's regiment, then under the command of Lieutenant Henry B. Beecher. The Eighteenth Corps was a part of the Union forces moving on Cold Harbor, Virginia, and participated in battles there on June 3–4, 1864. Hillers's unit subsequently participated in the siege of Petersburg from mid-June 1864 to early April 1865. Finally, in the closing days of the war, Hillers moved with his unit into Richmond.[6]

After the war ended, Hillers's company remained in Virginia until October 1865, when it was transferred to Fort Delaware, Delaware. There Hillers became a corporal in May 1866 and a sergeant in September of the same year. He was discharged at Fort Delaware on February 2, 1867,

"by expiration of service as a Sergeant." He presumably returned to New York City but must not have found conditions to his liking. On May 28, 1867, he reenlisted in the army at Fort Warren, Massachusetts, and was assigned to Company K of the Third Artillery. He was promoted to corporal the following month, and sergeant three months later. He served at Fort Warren for an undetermined period and was then assigned to Fort McAllister, near Savannah, Georgia. There, on May 28, 1870, again "by expiration of service as a Sergeant," Hillers was discharged from the U.S. Army for a third time. While in Georgia he courted a "young widow" but managed to retain his "bachelor's resolution," as he later wrote.[7]

Hillers apparently returned again to New York City, but soon thereafter he joined his brother, Richard M. Hillers, who was working as a blacksmith in San Francisco.[8] Jack remained in San Francisco until the spring of 1871. If the family legend is correct, he probably left San Francisco around May 10, 1871, stopped in Salt Lake City to seek work—and found it with John Wesley Powell.

Hillers may already have responded to the charisma and determination of the slight, bearded man whom everyone called "the Major," from his Union army rank. The path John Wesley Powell had followed to Green River City was a circuitous one. Born March 24, 1834, in Mt. Morris, New York, Powell was the fourth of nine children of recently emigrated English parents, Joseph and Mary Dean Powell. Joseph was an itinerant farmer, tailor, and Methodist circuit-riding preacher. From New York the Powells moved successively westward, finally settling in western Illinois. Young Powell became fascinated with geology, fossils, and Indian artifacts. He acquired a smattering of college learning but was largely self-educated. In 1854 he began to teach school.

When the Civil War began Powell enlisted as a private, but soon became an officer and subsequently found himself on U.S. Grant's staff. In late 1861 Grant gave Powell leave to go to Detroit and marry his first cousin, Emma Dean. At Shiloh, in April 1862, Powell lost his right arm just below the elbow to a Confederate minie ball. Nursed back to health by Emma, who under a "perpetual pass" from General Grant was with Powell throughout the war, he returned to the fighting. He was at the long siege of Vicksburg. There, during lulls in the action, Powell and John Steward (who would come along on the second river trip) hunted fossils in the side walls of the trenches.

Discharged with the rank of major, Powell became a professor of natural history, first at Illinois Wesleyan University and then at Illinois Normal University. Turning his eyes westward as *the* place to do science and possibly gain fame, Powell led two expeditions to the Rocky Mountains in Colorado in 1867 and 1868. During the second trip he and Emma wintered along the White River in northwest Colorado. There Powell began his studies of Indians among a band of Utes camped nearby. He also explored along the canyons of the upper Green River, and concluded that the Green and Colorado rivers could be run in boats. Even at that late date the Canyon Country south of the Uintah Basin in Utah and north of the foot of the Grand Canyon in western Arizona was marked "unexplored" on maps. There were rumors that the Colorado disappeared in huge whirlpools into the earth, to emerge somewhere down canyon. Powell thought not. He returned east, secured the necessary backing in Illinois and from the Smithsonian Institution, had four boats built to his specifications, recruited a crew, and set out to make his first river trip.[9]

He began at Green River City, a division point for the Union Pacific Railroad where it spanned the Green River. On May 10, 1869, at Promontory Point, Utah, the Union Pacific and the Central Pacific lines had joined, completing the long-dreamed-of transcontinental railroad. A few days later, a westbound train had stopped at the Green River siding and uncoupled a flatcar carrying Powell's boats. On May 24, 1869, Powell and ten men in four boats had pushed off into the unknown. Three perilous months and 1,500 river miles later, Powell and six men in two boats emerged bedraggled but alive at the foot of the Grand Canyon to find men searching for their remains. They had endured rapids, smashed boats, near-starvation, and desertion, but they had run the Green and Colorado rivers—the first to do so.[10] The trip made Powell a hero, and he took advantage of the notoriety to gain a Congressional appropriation to continue exploration of the Colorado River system and the surrounding Canyon Country.

Now in 1871, Powell was back at the Green River bridge with three new, better-designed boats and a new crew, including Hillers. Powell now knew that the rivers could be run. There was still danger, but the second trip was much more of a scientific and topographic expedition than high adventure as the first had been. The previous year he had scouted the surrounding country and ar-

ranged for supply drops along the river at accessible points. With such backup Powell and his men could concentrate on geological studies, making an accurate topographic map, and photographing, for the first time, the wonders of the Canyon Country.[11]

With his Congressional appropriation, Powell's 1871 trip inaugurated what became the fourth of the so-called "Great Surveys," which explored, studied, and mapped large segments of the American West between 1867 and 1878. As the Civil War ended, many veterans and others turned toward and participated in what Wallace Stegner has called the "second opening" of the West. By 1867 the long-planned transcontinental railroad was abuilding. The California gold rush of the 1850s and the Comstock boom of the 1860s in Nevada kindled hopes of similar strikes elsewhere. Thousands flocked into the Rockies seeking gold and silver. Other thousands headed westward to take up farms, run cattle, or exploit vast timber resources. Manifest Destiny was shifting into high gear, for a second time.

Some men, such as Clarence King and Ferdinand Vandiveer Hayden and their associates, saw the West in a different light, as a place to do new and exciting science. A quarter or more of a continent awaited scientific studies of all sorts, from botany to zoology. The geology and topography of the country needed description and mapping, so that resources could be located for exploitation and land could be platted and taken up for farms and ranches. The rationale for establishing the four "Geological and Geographical" surveys was clear to many in government. And there was precedent. Ever since Lewis and Clark at the beginning of the nineteenth century, the federal government had sent expeditions to the West. Between 1813 and the Civil War, most of that work had been undertaken by the U.S. Army, especially the Corps of Topographical Engineers. Now, in the post–Civil War period, Congress turned to civilians. In 1867 it funded two civilian-directed surveys, led by Clarence King and F. V. Hayden. To keep its hand in, the army established its own survey, led by Lieutenant George M. Wheeler. Powell came last on the scene in 1870.

By 1871 the other surveys had staked out large areas of the West. The King Survey, officially the United States Geological Survey of the Fortieth Parallel, centered along a transect from California to Nebraska encompassing the transcontinental railroad corridor. King had previously worked for the California Geological Survey under Josiah

Dwight Whitney. Like Powell a bit later, King came to appreciate the value of photography in geological studies, especially through the work of Carleton E. Watkins, who was with the California Survey between 1865 and 1867. When King gained a Congressional appropriation to establish his own survey in 1867, he hired a "wet plate artist," Timothy H. O'Sullivan. O'Sullivan was a veteran of the photographic teams under Mathew Brady that produced the magnificent and horrifying visual documentation of the Civil War. O'Sullivan worked for King from 1867 through 1869, and possibly again briefly in 1870.[12]

The army survey, under Wheeler, officially the United States Geographical and Geological Survey West of the 100th Meridian, ranged widely over Nevada, California, Arizona, and New Mexico. Timothy O'Sullivan was Wheeler's photographer in 1871 and from 1873 to 1875. William Bell was Wheeler's photographer in 1872.[13]

The Hayden Survey, officially the United States Geological and Geographical Survey of the Territories, centered its activities in the Rocky Mountains and adjacent plains. F. V. Hayden had served with federal surveys before the Civil War. In 1870 he hired, "for kit and keep," a young photographer from Omaha, Nebraska, named William Henry Jackson. The following year, Hayden, Jackson, the landscape artist Thomas Moran, and others made their famous trek of discovery into the Yellowstone region. Jackson remained with the Hayden Survey until late 1878, during which time he produced a truly remarkable series of photographs of scenery, Indians, and archaeological sites in the West.[14] Hayden's use of photographs for publicity purposes, and as gifts to influential Congressmen, helped convince Powell of the utility of photography for purposes other than the strictly scientific.

Powell's survey had various official names, including the United States Geological and Geographical Survey of the Territories (Second Division) (Hayden's was the First Division), but it was most commonly known as the United States Geological and Geographical Survey of the Rocky Mountain Region. Powell began using photography by hiring E. O. Beaman in May 1871. Beaman was a professional photographer who came to Powell on the recommendation of the E. and M. T. Anthony Photographic Supply Company of New York.

Photography and Western Exploration

The four Great Surveys were not the first federally sponsored surveys and expeditions to use photography, although they were the first to do so with a modicum of success. The practice had antecedents in the use of expeditionary artists, beginning with the 1819 expedition to the Rocky Mountains under the command of Lieutenant Stephen H. Long, who were employed to sketch the country and the people. Titian Ramsay Peale, Samuel Seymour, and, later, Richard and Edward Kern, Balduin Möllhausen, and others accompanied the Topographical Engineers westward. The drawings and paintings they produced provided the major visual records of the West until after the Civil War.[15]

There were early attempts to use photography by federal explorers soon after the process of daguerreotypy became available in 1839. The intrepid John Charles Fremont carried a daguerreotype outfit on his first western expedition in 1842, but failed to achieve any results.[16] W. C. Mayhew, with Lieutenant Lorenzo Sitgreaves during a boundary survey in Indian Territory in 1850, made several daguerreotypes of the survey party. The artist John Mix Stanley, with the 1850s Pacific Railroad survey along the northern route, made daguerreotypes of some Rocky Mountain Indians in 1853. The same year, Solomon Nunes Carvalho accompanied Fremont on his fifth expedition and made numerous daguerreotypes, only one possible example of which survives.[17]

In 1859, the landscape painter Albert Bierstadt and a daguerreotypist, S. F. Frost, accompanied Frederick West Lander on a wagon road survey through South Pass on the Oregon Trail. One or two daguerreotypes have survived from this expedition. They reflect the limitations of daguerreotypy for recording landscapes. These limitations are well described by Captain James Hervey Simpson, who attempted to use daguerreotype equipment during his wagon road survey across the Great Basin, also in 1859:

I carried out with me a photographic apparatus, carefully supplied with the necessary chemicals by Mr. E. Anthony of New York, and a couple of gentlemen accompanied me as photographers; but although they took a large number of views, some of which have been the originals from which a few [illustrations] accompanying my journals have been derived, yet, as a general thing, the project proved a failure. Indeed, I am informed that in several Government expeditions a photographic apparatus has been an accompaniment, and that in every instance, and even with operators of undoubted skill, the enterprise has been attended with failure. The cause lies in some degree in the difficulty, in the field, at short notice, of having the preparations perfect enough to insure good pictures, but chiefly in the fact that the camera is not adapted to distant scenery. For objects close at hand . . . and for single portraits of persons and small groups, it does very well; but as, on exploring expeditions, the chief *desideratum* is to daguerreotype extensive mountain-chains and other notable objects having considerable extent, the camera has to be correspondingly distant to take in the whole field, and the consequence is a want of sharpness of outline, and in many instances, on account of the focal distance not being the same for every object within the field of view, a blurred effect, as well as distortion of parts. In my judgment, the camera is not adapted to explorations in the field, and a good artist, who can sketch readily and accurately, is much to be preferred.[18]

Perhaps mindful of the limitations of daguerreotypy, Lieutenant Joseph Christmas Ives tried the then-new wet-plate process during his explorations of the lower Colorado River by steamboat in 1857. But high winds destroyed the dark tent and the apparatus and no results were obtained.[19]

Daguerreotypy, a process of producing permanent images on small sheets of silver-plated copper, had shown the world the possibilities of photography. But the process had limitations, besides the problem of using it for landscapes that Simpson so eloquently lamented. The surfaces of daguerreotypes were such that images could only be seen well, or at all, under certain lighting conditions. The images were reversed, the sizes of the plates were quite small, exposure time was several minutes, and duplicate copies of a plate could not be made.

During the 1830s, several persons besides L. J. M. Daguerre struggled with the problem of fixing a permanent "photographic" image onto some suitable material.[20] In England, William H. F. Talbot and Sir John Herschel both worked on processes of coating paper with silver nitrate and exposing the paper to light to capture an image. These paper "plates" could be copied. The copying process, in effect, re-reversed the image, that is, "righted" the image and made light areas appear light and dark areas dark. In a paper published in 1839, Herschel used the term "photography" (although he may not have coined it) to describe this process. In 1840 he did coin the terms "negative" for the original plate produced in the camera and "positive" for the copy, or print, made from the negative.

The use of "Talbotypes" (or calotypes), as this process was generally called, solved some problems of the daguerreotype: the positive could be seen under any lighting conditions, the image was not reversed, and many copies could be made from a single negative. However, the quality of the daguerreotype images was much superior to that of talbotypes because talbotype negatives were made of paper. The fine detail captured on the polished silver daguerreotype surfaces could not be duplicated on rough-textured paper surfaces. Recognizing the problem, Herschel as early as 1839 had experimented with coating glass plates with a light-sensitive silver solution. But here a problem was getting the solution to stick to the glass. Several experimenters in Europe and America worked on this problem throughout the 1840s. One fairly successful "sticking agent" or medium was albumen (egg white). Photographs (called halotypes) using albumen-coated glass negatives, and positives printed on both paper and glass, were shown at the great Crystal Palace Exhibition in London in 1851. Also in 1851, Frederick Scott Archer, an English artist and photographer, described a process using collodion as the medium to hold a light-sensitive silver compound to a glass plate. Collodion quickly superseded albumen as a "sticking agent" and was the key to wet-plate process photography, the process used by Hillers and the other photographers of the Great Surveys.

Collodion was made by dissolving nitrated cotton (gun cotton) in alcohol and ether. A soluble iodide was then added to the solution. When the photographer was ready to take a picture, the syrupy collodion was flowed evenly onto a clean glass plate, a technique requiring some manipulative skill. The alcohol and ether quickly evaporated, leaving a thin whitish film on the glass. The collodion could be applied to the plate in daylight. The plate was then taken into a light-tight tent, or darkroom, and placed in a solution of silver nitrate for about one minute. The silver nitrate bath formed a light-sensitive silver iodide compound on the collodion film. The sensitized plate was then placed in a plate holder. If used while wet, the plate retained its light-sensitivity, but lost it if the plate dried during use. The plate holder was inserted into a previously aimed and focused camera. The camera lens was uncapped for several seconds to many minutes, depending upon ambient light and the aperture of the lens.

After exposure the plate was returned to the dark tent, or darkroom, and developed in a solution either of ferrous sulfate mixed with acetic acid or of pyrogallic acid. The negative was then "fixed" in a dilute solution either of potassium cyanide or of "hypo" (sodium thiosulfate). The former solution was thought to produce more contrastive tones on the negative. The negative was washed in clear water, dried, and often varnished to protect the emulsion. Negatives could then be stored until the photographer was ready to make positives. Prints were made by placing the negatives in a frame against a sheet of sensitized albumen-coated paper. The frame was exposed to sunlight for fifteen to thirty minutes. The print was developed in one of the same solutions used for negatives, then fixed, washed, dried, and mounted.[21]

The cumbersomeness of the wet-plate process, especially when used in the field, is apparent simply from the description. At each locale the photographer had to set up the tripod, aim and focus the camera, set up the dark tent and chemicals, coat the plate, make the exposure, develop and process the negative, take down the equipment, repack it in a wagon, on pack animals, or on his own back, and move on to the next point. Not only was the wet-plate process cumbersome, but so was the equipment. The photographic equipment E. O. Beaman brought for Powell's 1871 river trip weighed well over a thousand pounds, most of it glass plates for negatives. The equipment used by Beaman (and later Hillers) was similar to that of other photographers of the time: two (and sometimes more) cameras, a dark tent, chemicals and processing trays, and appropriately sized glass plates and plate holders for each camera.

For his overland work in the 1870s and 1880s Hillers used pack animals, and sometimes wagons, to carry his equipment. He did not use a horse-drawn ambulance converted to a darkroom on wheels, nor specially built "photographic vans," as did many of his private-practice contemporaries. Such vans were a familiar sight in many parts of the country from the 1860s on. Since Hillers was based in Washington, D.C., after 1873 but photographed in widely separate places, such a convenience was obviously out of the question. The dark tent Hillers used, at least in the early 1870s, was probably a Carbutt's Portable Developing Box. The dark tent appearing in Beaman photographs of the 1871 river trip (fig. 1), and in a picture of Hillers on the Aquarius Plateau in Utah in 1875 (fig. 54), is very similar to illustrations of the Carbutt Box. In his early work Hillers used three sizes of cameras: 5 × 8 inch and 8 × 10 inch view cameras and a stereo camera. He

does not seem to have used a stereo camera much later than 1879. In later years he used an 11 × 14 inch view camera. His classic photographs of the southwestern pueblos, Canyon de Chelly, and the Yosemite Valley were made with an 11 × 14 camera. He also used a smaller 5 × 8 camera for detailed work.

Large-format cameras were required to produce large-format photographs, since no practical way of making positive enlargements from negatives was invented until the 1880s. Some view cameras took glass plates as large as 20 × 24 inches. Carleton Watkins used a camera of his own design of about that size as early as 1861 in California. Charles L. Weed used a similar-sized camera in 1864–65 in Yosemite Valley, as did Eadweard Muybridge in 1872. In 1875 W. H. Jackson lugged such a monster, probably a Semmindinger "mammoth plate" wet-collodion camera, up and down the canyons and mesas of southwestern Colorado while he photographed landscapes and "Cliff Dweller" archaeological sites. Such mammoth cameras were extremely heavy and cumbersome, as were the glass plates used in them. Also, evenly coating such large plates with collodion was very difficult. Hence, most large-format cameras used by federal survey photographers, and by others in the 1870s, were in the size range used by Hillers: 5 × 8, 8 × 10, and occasionally 11 × 14 inches.[22]

When we remember that Hillers, Jackson, O'Sullivan, Watkins, and others carried their heavy cameras and dark tents up mountain peaks and down canyon bottoms, their photographic achievements become even more remarkable.

Down the Colorado

At 6:00 A.M., May 16, 1871, a day after his meeting with Powell in Salt Lake City, Hillers found himself at Green River City. Like others on the trip, Hillers kept a diary. In it he wrote that the population of Green River City consisted of "about 100 persons, whites, mongolian, and copper-colored."[23] He also found an interesting group of new companions. Hillers listed them in his diary, and E. O. Beaman took their photograph (fig. 1) in the boats: "The whole party stands as follows: Major Powell, Geologist; Prof. Thompson, Astronomer and Topographer; Bishop (Cap) and Jones (Deacon), Assistents; Steward, Assistent Geologist; Beaman, Photographer; Clement

Powell, Assistent; Dellenbaugh, Artist; Frank Richardson, Barometrician; Hattan (General), Cook."[24]

Hillers was assigned to the *Emma Dean,* named for Powell's wife. Powell sat in a captain's chair that Hillers had strapped onto the boat, which allowed Powell to see ahead and spot rapids. Besides Powell and Hillers in the *Emma Dean,* there was Stephen Vandiver Jones, a school principal from Washburn, Illinois; A. H. Thompson had persuaded him to come along to aid in the mapping. In the bow was seventeen-year-old Frederick Samuel Dellenbaugh, a distant relative of Thompson's. Dellenbaugh and Hillers became fast friends.

In the *Nellie Powell,* named for Ellen Powell Thompson, was A. H. Thompson, Powell's brother-in-law. Thompson, a competent, steady man, was the expedition topographer and second in command. With Thompson was Francis Marion Bishop. He had been in the first Battle of Bull Run and at Antietam and was badly wounded at Fredericksburg in 1862. He emerged from the war with the rank of captain and had been a student of Powell's at Illinois Wesleyan University. John Steward was also in the *Nellie Powell.* He made most of the geological section drawings during the trip that were later used in Powell's classic monograph on the geology of the Canyon Country.[25] Little is known of Frank Richardson, the "supercargo." At the end of the first week, Powell thought him too weak to make the trip and sent him back to Green River City.

Steering the *Canonita* was E. O. Beaman, the expedition's first photographer. With Beaman was Andy Hattan, oarsman and, most importantly, cook for the expedition. Also aboard was Powell's first cousin, Walter Clement (Clem) Powell. The plan was for cousin Clem to learn photography, but he could not master it and left the expedition at the end of 1872.[26]

Starting in Photography

Soon after the river trip began, Hillers became interested in photography. He volunteered to help Beaman by carrying the heavy equipment up and down cliffs and talus slopes. He became increasingly interested as the trip progressed.[27] F. S. Dellenbaugh, in a letter written in 1932 to the photographic historian Robert Taft, detailed the development of Hillers's interest:

Jack Hillers was engaged by Powell for the second trip, in Salt Lake City, to pull an oar and to help generally. He then knew nothing about photography, but he became much interested as we went down the Green River.

When we had arrived at the mouth of the Green . . . Hillers asked me about photography—about the chemical side. I explained about the action of the light on a glass plate coated with collodion and sensitized with nitrate of silver, the bath to eliminate the silver in hypo, and so on.

"Why couldn't I do that?" he said. I replied that he certainly could, for he was a careful, cleanly man, and those were the chief qualities needed. I advised him to offer help to Beaman whenever possible . . . and perhaps Beaman would let him try a negative. He did, and in two or three weeks had made such progress that he overshadowed Clement Powell.[28]

When the boating party reached the mouth of the Dirty Devil River at the head of Glen Canyon, one of the boats was cached. The intention was to retrieve it by an overland route the following spring. Hillers wrote: "October 1 [1871] Cached the *Canonita* until next spring, having no material for photographing [remaining] and are short of provisions. Major intends to explore this part of the country, bring in [photographic] material and ride down in her on the Colorado to the Par Weep [Paria River]."[29]

The 1871 portion of the boat trip down the Green and Colorado rivers ended at Lee's Ferry, Arizona (map 1) in late October. Powell and Hillers had disembarked at Crossing of the Fathers, fifty miles upstream, on October 10, traveling to Kanab, Utah, and then on to Salt Lake City, three hundred and fifty miles north. There they resupplied and prepared to bring Powell's wife Emma, new daughter Mary Dean, born while Powell was on the river, and his sister, Ellen Powell Thompson, back to Kanab. Meanwhile, A. H. Thompson established a base camp near Kanab, from which he could direct overland work on a map of the region.

In late January 1872 Powell and Beaman "had a falling out," as Hillers wrote in his diary. Beaman was paid off and discharged. Powell retained the rights to the photographs and stereographs Beaman had taken during the trip, as well as the photographic equipment.[30] On February 2, 1872, Hillers drove Powell, Emma, and baby Mary by wagon from Kanab to Beaver, Utah. From there the Powells took a stagecoach to Salt Lake City, then a train to Illinois and on to Washington, D.C., where Powell successfully sought a continuation of his Congressional appropriation.

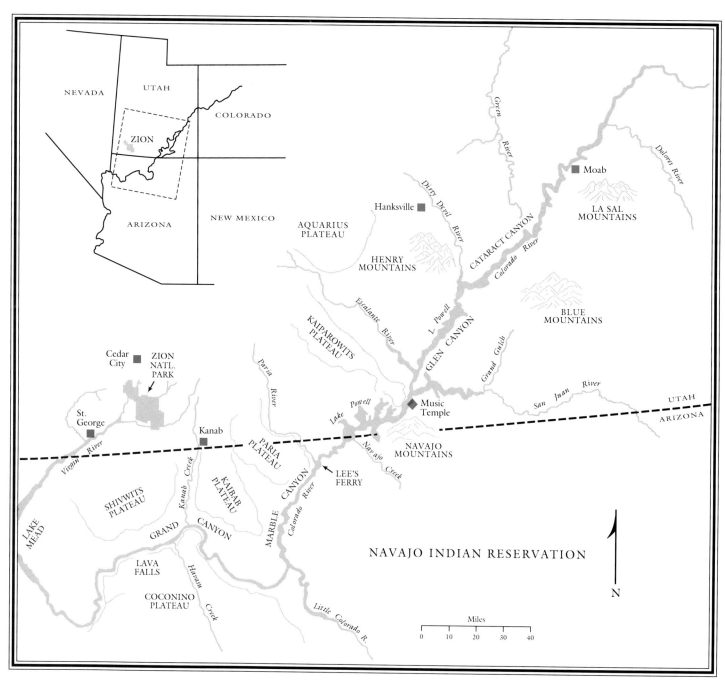

NEVADA
UTAH
COLORADO
ZION
ARIZONA
NEW MEXICO

Green River

Dolores River

Moab

Hanksville

Dirty Devil River

AQUARIUS
PLATEAU

HENRY
MOUNTAINS

CATARACT CANYON

LA SAL
MOUNTAINS

Colorado River

Escalante River

KAIPAROWITS
PLATEAU

L. Powell

GLEN CANYON

BLUE
MOUNTAINS

Grand Gulch

Cedar
City

ZION
NATL.
PARK

Paria River

Lake Powell

Music
Temple

San Juan River

UTAH
ARIZONA

St.
George

Kanab

PARIA
PLATEAU

Navajo Creek

NAVAJO
MOUNTAINS

Virgin River

Kanab Creek

KAIBAB
PLATEAU

MARBLE CANYON

Colorado River

LEE'S
FERRY

NAVAJO INDIAN RESERVATION

LAKE
MEAD

SHIVWITS
PLATEAU

GRAND

CANYON

N

LAVA
FALLS

Havasu Creek

COCONINO
PLATEAU

Little Colorado R.

Miles

0   10   20   30   40

MAP I. Lower Colorado River Region, Utah-Arizona.

Hillers returned to Kanab with orders to assist Clem Powell in taking photographs. While Hillers was gone, Clem proved to be inept. Dellenbaugh recalled: "When Beaman left at the end of our first season of river work, the photography fell on Clement. He made a trip with Hillers as assistant and returned with nothing. He declared that Beaman had put hypo in the developer. Beaman . . . said he had not done so—that the trouble was Clem's carelessness." On February 4, 1872, Thompson recorded that "Clem did not get pictures. For some reason his chemicals would not work. He thinks it is in the bath. Broke his camera all to bits. Horse fell off cliff and fell on it. Clem says the pictures would spot and fog." When Hillers returned, with another camera, the two made some "Views" on the Kaibab Plateau and in Kanab Canyon, where Hillers noted in his diary that they had "photographed all the best scenery."[31]

But the Major, with just cause, did not have full confidence in his new team, especially in cousin Clem. On his way to Washington, D.C., Powell stopped in Salt Lake City and called upon Charles R. Savage, of the photographic firm of Savage and Ottinger. The previous October, Powell had brought Beaman's stereographs to the firm to be printed. The work was done by a young assistant, James Fennemore. Powell remembered Fennemore and in February 1872 hired him to go to Kanab and take over the photographic duties.

Meanwhile, Clem and Hillers had made their first successful foray. On March 11, 1872, A. H. Thompson wrote to Powell from Pipe Springs, Arizona: "We have just arrived here from the Kaibab [Plateau]. . . . Clem and Jack are doing well photographing. Got over 30 views from Kaibab and Kanab Canon. I think 20 of them are good. . . . Clem and Jack can make pictures I think, especially Jack. When we get Mr. Fennimore we shall be pretty strong in the picture department."[32]

Fennemore arrived on March 19 and he, Thompson, Clem, Hillers, and others went to the Mt. Trumbull area on the North Rim of the Grand Canyon. Both Hillers and Clem assisted Fennemore with the photography. Dellenbaugh recalled that Fennemore "was an excellent photographer and a genial fellow. . . . He was good to Hillers and gave him much instruction, with the result that Hillers became expert in the work, became assistant, in fact."[33]

On April 25, Hillers wrote to Powell from Berry Springs, Utah:

I returned to Kanab from Beaver, just in time to take a trip to the Buckskins [Kaibab Plateau]. Clem and myself made Pictures of the Canon and Stewards [Levi Stewart's] Ranch, then started down the Kanab Wash. Made some 25 views then returned to Pipe Springs where the Party was fitting up for Mount Trumbull. Here Mr. Fenemore joined us and took charge. On the 21st of March we started for Trumbull. Jones and [Pardyn] Dodds started for the [Colorado] River but could find no place to go down to the bank of the River with animals. On their return Jones and Fenemore started back for Kanab to rejoin us at this place (Foot of Pine Valley Mt.). I took the Instruments and started for the River to try my hand. While going down a Lava Gulch, I discovered some Hieroglyphics which I copied with the Camera. On reaching the River it began to storm which continued for three days. I had to start back disappointed. I made two Pictures near a Picket at which we camped. . . . On the 12th of the Month, Capt. Dodds, Fred[erick Dellenbaugh], Fenemore and myself started back to finish up. Made 25 pictures. I tell you Major they are Grand. . . . Fen[nemore] made a Picture showing the whole Canon. For this purpose we climbed half way down—showing the River for nearly three miles and the walls 2000 feet below and 3000 feet above. It will look grand in a "scope" [i.e., a stereopticon viewer].[34]

The photograph that Hillers refers to is shown in figure 2, a view of the Inner Gorge of the Grand Canyon. The man on the cliff is Hillers. The party also descended to the river at Lava Falls and made several shots of the rapids (fig. 3), the mightiest in the Grand Canyon. From the Grand Canyon, Hillers and Fennemore turned northward toward the Kolob Plateau, the massive southern extension of the Wasatch Plateaus. The Kolob is incised by the North Fork of the Virgin River, which has carved out the breathtaking wonders of Zion Canyon. The East Fork of the Virgin flows through Parunuweap Canyon to converge with the North Fork just below the present-day entrance to Zion National Park. Again they photographed the spectacular scenery, including Hillers again lying on a ledge overlooking the view (fig. 4).

Through Glen Canyon

The 1871 river party had cached one of the boats, the Canonita, at the mouth of the Dirty Devil River, which marks the head of Glen Canyon. The plan was to take a pack train overland, retrieve the boat, float leisurely through Glen Canyon (there were few serious rapids between the Dirty Devil and Lee's Ferry), and take photographs. Pow-

2. *View of Grand Canyon from Lava*, April 1872. J. K. Hillers on ledge. James Fennemore photograph. National Archives photo no. 57-PS-61 (Geological Survey Collection).

3. Lava Falls rapids in Grand Canyon, April 19 or 20, 1872. Fennemore and Hillers tried to capture the swirl and roar of the rapids. This photograph is a remarkable feat, given the slow exposure time demanded by the equipment. James Fennemore and Jack Hillers photograph. National Archives photo no. 57-PS-618 (Geological Survey Collection).

4. *Mukuntuweap Valley* (Zion Canyon), Utah, April 1872. J. K. Hillers on ledge. James Fennemore photograph. National Archives photo no. 57-PS-67 (Geological Survey Collection).

5. Caulking the *Canonita* at the mouth of the Dirty Devil River, Utah, June 23-24, 1872. Left to right: W. D. Johnson, Jr., F. S. Dellenbaugh, J. K. Hillers. James Fennemore photograph. National Archives photo no. 57-PS-778 (Geological Survey Collection).

ell recognized its spectacular and haunting beauty and wanted to add a Glen Canyon series to the photographic and stereographic collection.[35] The trip would bring the boat to Lee's Ferry, where the other boats were cached, in time for the planned second leg of the river trip through Marble and Grand canyons.

On May 20, 1872, Thompson wrote Powell from Kanab:

We start for the Dirty Devil day after tomorrow. . . . Think now that the boat can leave the "creek" about June 6th. Four weeks coming down. Take 150 glass. Have had Fennemore and Jack print from negatives taken on Mt. Trumbull and of the Virgin. . . . Had some mounted. Send you about 30 by this mail. Think Fennemore's pictures are very frosty—generally he overexposes and overdevelops [see figs. 2 and 4] . . . I think he will take much better pictures after this. My object in printing and mounting was to enable him to see his work. . . . Jack is getting along nicely. Took no. 20 [of those sent to Powell] alone some time ago. Jack is quite anxious that you should arrange it that he can work at photography through Grand Canon. I had rather have Jack (if he had more experience) than Beaman, Fennemore and Clem combined. Will work harder and select better, more characteristic and artistic views.[36]

Thompson, Hillers, Dellenbaugh, Fennemore, and others started for the Dirty Devil River on May 25. The pack trip took them across the Aquarius Plateau and through the Henry Mountains, one peak of which Thompson named for Hillers. Fennemore was sick during part of the trek across the Aquarius (the 9,000 to 11,000 foot altitude may not have helped). Hillers did some of the photography, including shots of Bee and Aspen lakes.[37] Finally, after much searching for a route, the party reached the mouth of the Dirty Devil.[38] The *Canonita* was recovered, caulked, and painted (fig. 5). On June 26, 1872, Hillers, Fennemore, Dellenbaugh, and William D. Johnson, Jr., set off through "Mound" and "Monument" canyons (the two were subsequently grouped together as "Glen Canyon" by Powell). Hillers assisted Fennemore in taking numerous photographs in Glen Canyon and its side canyons (e.g., fig. 6). Along the way, the party camped in the cavernous Music Temple, a large alcove in the Navajo sandstone formation, just downstream from the confluence of the San Juan and Colorado rivers. Powell and crew had camped there in 1869, had sung songs and, appreciating the acoustics, had given the alcove its name. There two of the 1869 crew, O. C. Howland and William H. Dunn, had carved their names on the alcove wall. In 1871 the second

6. Side canyon in Glen Canyon, Colorado River, Utah, probably July 2, 1872. James Fennemore and Jack Hillers photograph. National Archives photo no. 57-PS-779 (Geological Survey Collection).

river party had stopped at Music Temple to lunch, and Dellenbaugh and Bishop added their names while Hillers carved Powell's name. In 1872 Dellenbaugh added a "—72" to his name and date and Hillers carved his name and date.[39]

The *Canonita* arrived at Lee's Ferry on July 13, 1872. The crew waited a month before Powell and various visitors turned up. Hillers kept himself busy cleaning negative glass and helping John D. Lee and two of Lee's five wives, who were hiding with him in the isolated place. Lee was a prominent Mormon who had been an early convert in 1839. He had gone to Utah in 1848 and ultimately was directed to settle in southern Utah. He was involved in the infamous Mountain Meadows Massacre in September 1857, west of Cedar City, Utah, in which a group of Mormons, and perhaps some Indians, killed the members of a non-Mormon emigrant party bound for California. By 1872 Lee had become the principal national scapegoat for the affair. He was excommunicated by the Mormon Church in 1871, but was also directed to go into hiding. He chose the confluence of the Paria and Colorado rivers, Lonely Dell, as he aptly called it. He took Rachel Woolsey Lee and Emma Bachellor Lee with him. The confluence was one of the few places where the Colorado River could be crossed. Lee built a ferry, and "Lee's Ferry," rather than Lonely Dell, ultimately became the name of the place.[40]

When Hillers, Fennemore, Dellenbaugh, and Johnson arrived at the confluence, Emma Lee agreed to cook for them, and did so to their delight. Fennemore fell ill and Emma nursed him for three weeks, to his great gratitude. He recovered, but only enough to conclude that he could not stand the rigors of the Grand Canyon boat trip. Hillers spent much time with Lee during the month of waiting for Powell. He thought Lee was a splendid fellow, but wrote in his diary that he did not change his negative opinion of Mormonism in general.[41] Lee finally "confessed participation as leader" of the massacre, as it says on the plaque at the site. On March 23, 1877, nearly twenty years after the massacre, John D. Lee was executed at Mountain Meadows. Ironically, it was James Fennemore who took a famous photograph of Lee seated on his own coffin awaiting his demise.

When the boat trip started, Fennemore returned to Salt Lake City. He subsequently opened his own photographic establishment in the city and operated it for many years. He died in 1941, aged ninety-one, the last survivor of the Powell river expeditions. As W. C. Darrah notes, "Fennemore's most important service to the Powell expedition was his patient instruction of Jack Hillers."[42]

Marble and Grand Canyons

With Fennemore unable to continue, Powell concluded to take only one photographic outfit instead of two, and put Hillers, not cousin Clem, in charge of it. Hillers, henceforth, was to be the Powell Survey photographer, and Powell's principal photographer for many years thereafter. As the boats left from Lonely Dell and turned downstream into the mouth of Marble Canyon, Hillers's brief but intense photographic apprenticeship was over. He was faced with making photographs of some of the world's most spectacular scenery, under the most difficult of circumstances. He was up to the task. During the arduous run through Marble Canyon and on into Grand Canyon, Hillers took many excellent photographs (e.g., figs. 7, 9–11).[43] The main problem Hillers encountered was aggravating his old back injury from Civil War days; the injury plagued him for the rest of his life.

When the boating party reached the mouth of Kanab Canyon, on September 7, 1872, they were met by packers who had brought supplies. Two days later, Hillers wrote, "Quite a surprise at breakfast. Major told us that our voyage of toil and danger was at an end on the river. Everyone felt like praising God."[44] Some major and very difficult rapids (even for modern inflatable rafts) lay ahead. The boats and the men were badly worn. Powell concluded that further mapping and geological studies could be conducted overland. And Hillers had obtained a magnificent set of views of the Grand Canyon from river level. Further risk was not justified.

Most of the party returned to Kanab to continue the mapping. Hillers and Clem Powell remained in the canyon a few days to take more photographs, for example figures 9–11.

To the Hopi Mesas

On October 9, 1872, Hillers, Clem Powell, Andy Hattan, and the famed Mormon explorer and Indian missionary Jacob Hamblin set out from Kanab for the Hopi mesas in

7. Marble Canyon above mouth of Nankoweap Canyon, looking upriver, August 22, 1872. National Archives photo no. 57-PS-854 (Geological Survey Collection).

8. Repairing boats at the foot of Granite Rapid, Grand Canyon, September 1, 1872. F. S. Dellenbaugh on left; others unidentified. Dana Butte in center distance. National Archives photo no. 57-PS-871 (Geological Survey Collection).

9. *The Abandoned Boats,* Kanab Canyon, Arizona, September 10, 1872. The *Canonita* and the *Emma Dean* are shown. Hillers wrote, "Came back [from the river] and made a picture of the dismantled boats." The Denver Public Library, Western History Department.

10. Marble Pinnacle, Kanab Canyon, Arizona, September 15, 1872. Hillers wrote, "The canon often doubles on itself, leaving only a thin wall in the bend. Photographed one to-day measuring in height over 2000 ft., all marble, measuring through its base only about 200 feet," National Archives photo no. 57-PS-71 (Geological Survey Collection).

11. Field of prickly pear (*Opuntia*) cactus, Kanab Canyon, Arizona, September 15, 1872. Hillers noted, "Lots of cactus apples grow all along the side of the canon—eat lots of them every day. They are a delicious fruit and I think very healthy." National Archives photo no. 57-PS-578 (Geological Survey Collection).

Arizona. Their purposes were to photograph the Hopi people and their villages and to purchase artifacts for the Smithsonian Institution. They crossed the Colorado River at Lee's Ferry, then turned southeast to the Hopi mesas, arriving on October 23. Clem notes on November 1, 1872, "Pictures have not been a success but the impressions will be good to engrave from." Hillers's diary is less optimistic: "Tried photographing but the traps were out of order." William V. Jones's diary notes that Hillers and Clem had returned to Kanab on November 21: "Had a good trip but made no pictures." It is regrettable that Hillers and Clem did not succeed in bringing back the photographs Clem's diary indicates they took. On October 29, he notes, "During the afternoon we succeeded in making one or two instantaneous views of the [women's] dances" on First Mesa.[45] These would probably have been the first-ever photographs of Hopi ceremonial dances, in this instance those of the women's Oaqol society, which dances in October. In later years photographers would elbow each other out of the way in their attempts to record Hopi ceremonial dances, particularly the dramatic Snake and Flute dances.[46]

The artifact purchases went much better. Clem records that a "nice assortment of pottery, baskets, skins, moccasins, leggings, etc." was acquired.[47] The artifacts were laboriously carried by pack mule to Kanab, then by wagon to Salt Lake City, thence by railroad to the Smithsonian.

Soon after Hillers and Clem returned to Kanab, the Powell party was visited by one of the survey teams from the rival Wheeler Expedition. Relations were cordial but cool, since in a sense territorial rights and scientific prerogatives were being tested by the Wheeler party. Among the visitors were the geologist Grove Karl Gilbert and the photographer William Bell. Undoubtedly, Gilbert and Powell talked—they had first met earlier in the season at Salt Lake City. The two continued to cross paths and obviously established a mutual regard. In late 1874 Gilbert left Wheeler and joined the Powell Survey.[48]

In the cold days of November 1872 in Kanab, Bell and Hillers, accompanied by Clem, exchanged visits to see each other's work and equipment. Clem noted that Bell showed them "how to develop dry plates; do not like the process as well as the wet."[49] Dry plates in the 1870s were still very experimental, and would remain so for another decade. Clem's preference was quite appropriate.

But there were lighter moments in the Powell Survey winter camp. Dellenbaugh, Hillers, and the others were occasionally entertained by the local Mormon families. But they also whiled away evenings talking and singing. Dellenbaugh composed a song, "Colorado Days," set to the music of a Confederate tune, "Then Farewell Forever to the Star Spangled Banner. No Longer May It Wave o'er the Land of the Free." The song bade farewell to the river-running days, and recalled Hillers's fondness for singing:

Oh, boys, you remember
The old Colorado
The *Nellie* and the *Dean*
And the *Canonita* too;
The portages and "let downs,"
The "blind box" and the "photos"
All flash through your minds
As do things of the past.

There's Andy and his kettles,
And Bish and his "threedolite,"
With Beaman pass before us
In our vision of old times;
The Major and Professor,
And Deacon Jones, no lesser,
And hearty "Uncle" Steward,
The exhorter of our band.

And Jack, our jolly songster,
The warbler of the "Aigles,"
Who sang us many "Zephyrs"
To cheer the lonely camp.
Still another must be mentioned,
He shall always be "Yours Truly,"
And the Zephyrs from the Canons
He dedicates to you.

Then farewell forever
To the wild Colorado;
Its rapids and its rocks
Will trouble us no more;
But we'll be free and merry,
Amidst old forms and faces,
While the great foaming river
Dashes on to the sea.

When Frederick Dellenbaugh, the last survivor of those who had run the Colorado with Powell, revisited southern Utah in 1919, he found the song still being sung.[50]

In December 1872 Hillers accompanied Major Powell, Clem, and others to Salt Lake City. The party stopped at Gunnison, Utah, to make arrangements for a base camp so that mapping of the Wasatch Plateaus could continue from that locale the following year. Clem Powell left the expedition and returned to Illinois. Major Powell went on to Washington to see to further appropriations for his survey.

Hillers purchased supplies and then returned to Kanab, Utah, on January 1, 1873, to make photographs and assist Thompson with the mapping work. With an Indian guide, Hillers spent three weeks in January and early February 1873 in the Mt. Trumbull region on the North Rim of the Grand Canyon. He was able to make only a dozen photographs, but they include some of his classic views of the Grand Canyon.[51] Thompson moved the survey camp to Gunnison in mid-April 1873. Earlier that month, Hillers again visited the Virgin River area and made photographs in Zion and Parunuweap canyons (figs. 12–14). Hillers had first visited the Zion Canyon area during his trip onto the Kolob Plateau with Fennemore the previous year. Now he was back to add a "Virgin River Series" of photographs and stereographs. By April 1873, enough of Beaman's, Fennemore's, Clem Powell's, and Hillers's photographs had accumulated that they were divided into regional series. This allowed the production of stereographs in sets, which were being sold through several commercial outlets in the East. Ultimately, Green River, Mound [Glen] Canyon, Grand Canyon, Virgin River, Bullion Canyon, and various sets on Indians were produced.

Hillers did some of his best early work during the April 1873 trip. He was helped by the spectacular scenery, but one can see in the photographs an assured sense of composition and a balanced use of light and reflections. Contemporary art historians see in his Virgin River and other later works elements of the luminist tradition so popular among many nineteenth-century landscape painters and photographers.[52] When Hillers had completed his "Virgin Views," he wrote Powell a letter that reflects his increasing confidence as a photographer:

"All good things come slow," so did the long wished for Views of the Grand Canon and Kanab Wash. I am pleased with a good many, but some are not up to the mark. I see where my faults lies, will try to avoid them in future. This whole batch are done

12. The Three Patriarchs, Parunuweap Canyon, Virgin River Valley, Utah, April 1873. The photograph was taken just downstream from the Narrows in Parunuweap Canyon and the (now abandoned) settlement of Shunesburg, Utah. National Archives photo no. 57-PS-64 (Geological Survey Collection).

13. *Reflected Tower, Rio Virgin, Utah*, April 1873. This is a view in Zion Canyon, or Mukuntuweap Canyon as Powell originally named it. It officially became Zion Canyon when the area was made a national park in the 1930s. National Archives photo no. 200S-JH-53 (Geological Survey Collection, Hillers's album).

14. Virgin River valley, below Zion Canyon, Utah, April or August 1873. The photograph shows the Virgin River valley below the confluence of the North and East forks of the river. Cultivated fields of the Mormon settlement of Virgin City appear in the lower left corner of the scene. National Archives photo no. 57-PS-80 (Geological Survey Collection).

middling for Greenhorns. I have done very little this winter in the Photo line. I have secured the views of Kanab Canon, no doubt you have seen them all but the Cave Lakes [a series of three pools in Kanab Canyon, upstream from the settlement of Kanab, Utah] which you can look at with the Virgen views. I have succeeded in printing the Virgen pictures a little better, but you know I have to find out everything by actual experiments. These pictures are not well mounted for I have no dies to cut them with, I have to guess at it. I would like to go up the Virgen again should any of us have our work up there. I was in the Narrows [Parunuweap Canyon] for four days but could stand it no longer. My body was blue every night. Water was too cold. Ice on the edges every morning. I went up eight bends. I am pleased with all the views I made in the Narrows. Prof. [A. H. Thompson] thinks that some of them are rich. I am deficient in printing them and cant get at the trick to clean the shadows.[53]

In order to get through the Parunuweap Narrows, Hillers had to wade in the river, hence his body being "blue" from the icy water. Following the Virgin River trip, Hillers returned to Gunnison in mid-May to rejoin A. H. Thompson. Thompson had begun mapping the high Wasatch Plateaus, which form the western edge of the Canyon Country in central Utah. The west slopes of the Plateaus are drained, in part, by the Sevier River, which flows to a desert lake terminus in the Great Basin. Hillers made a number of scenic shots along tributaries of the Sevier River (e.g., figs. 15–16), as well as a field portrait of A. H. Thompson (fig. 17) while he was working in the Gunnison region. Hillers was especially fond of Thompson—perhaps because Thompson had supported him over Clem Powell to become the expedition photographer. But Thompson clearly favored quality work over family ties. His diary of his years in Utah reflects that integrity in several instances.[54]

15. Pilling's Cascade, Bullion Canyon, Utah, May or June 1873. National Archives photo no. 57-PS-110A (Geological Survey Collection).

16. Nettle Creek, Utah, May or June 1873. National Archives photo no. 57-PS-683 (Geological Survey Collection).

17. Almon Harris Thompson, probably near Kanab, Utah, 1872 or 1873. National Archives photo no. 57-PS-633 (Geological Survey Collection).

Notes

1. Biographical data on Hillers's life before he met Powell are scanty. The information presented here derives from Hillers's military and pension records in the U.S. National Archives (cited as Hillers Records); from his marriage certificate; from an obituary in the Washington, D.C., *Star* dated Nov. 16, 1925; from Darrah, "Beaman, Fennemore, Hillers"; and from personal interviews by the present author with Hillers's daughter-in-law, the late Mrs. J. K. (Lila) Hillers, Jr., of Washington, D.C., in 1968 and 1972. I am grateful also for information provided, between 1977 and 1984, by Mrs. Dorothy McKenzie, of Fayetteville, Pennsylvania, Hillers's granddaughter, and Richard McKenzie, of Ross, California, Hillers's great-grandson.

Whether Hillers's christened middle name was Heinrich or Karl is unclear; certainly he used "K." throughout his life. Records in the Utah Genealogical Society of the Mormon Church, Salt Lake City, list a "Johann Karl Hillers" born near Hanover, Germany, on December 20, 1843. The major document in which "Heinrich" occurs is his marriage certificate (photocopy in the author's possession), which gives his name as "Johann Heinrich Hillers."

The reference to the Hillers family "possibly" stopping in Hull, England, for a time before continuing to the United States derives from two documents in Hillers Records. Late in his life, on June 1, 1915, Hillers signed an affidavit listing his date and place of birth as "Dec. 20, 1843, Hull, England." This is repeated in a surgeon's certificate filled out in 1920, but the latter is typed and apparently copied from the 1915 document. A typed memorandum from the Pensioner's Office, dated Jan. 3, 1914, gives Hillers's year of arrival in the U.S. as 1859, but this may well be a typographical error. There is no record in the files of the Utah Genealogical Society of a John K. (or a John H.) Hillers, or a person of any similar name, being born in Hull, England, in 1843, or in the several years before

or after that date. Given the available data, I conclude that Johann Karl Hillers was born in Brinkum, Hannover, Germany on Dec. 20, 1843, and that he may have spent some time in Hull, England, but emigrated with his family to New York City in 1852. As explained later, church records in New York City (other than Hillers's marriage certificate, a copy of which was obtained from Mrs. J. K. Hillers, Jr.) that may resolve the problem are not currently available.

2. Dellenbaugh, *Canyon Voyage*, pp. 75–76. Hillers apparently kept in touch with the "Aigles" in later years. In his diary entry for March 11, 1872, he noted getting letters from "all the 'aigles'" (Hillers, *Diary*, p. 99).

3. Hillers Records. This and subsequent Muster Roll citations are derived from summaries of Hillers's military records sent from the Adjutant General's Office of the War Department to the Commissioner of Pensions on June 10 and October 9, 1891.

4. Hillers, *Diary*, p. 136.

5. Hillers Records.

6. See Foote, *Civil War*, p. 740; Johnson and Buel, *Battles and Leaders of the Civil War*, 4:537–94; Long and Long, *Civil War Day by Day*, pp. 490–666.

7. Hillers, *Diary*, p. 170.

8. Hillers, *Diary*, pp. 10, 15, 142, 145.

9. For further biographical data on Powell see Darrah, *Powell of the Colorado*, Stegner, *Beyond the Hundredth Meridian*, and Fowler and Fowler, "John Wesley Powell, Anthropologist."

10. One man left the expedition early on. Three others left at Separation Rapid in the Grand Canyon just a few days before the end of the trip. They climbed out of the Canyon onto the North Rim and were killed by Indians. One boat was lost on the upper Green River and a second abandoned at Separation Rapid. For the 1869 river trip see the journals and letters in Darrah, "Biographical Sketches and Original Documents," Marston, "The Lost Journal of John Colton Sumner," and J. W. Powell, *Exploration of the*

Colorado River.

11. When the present author began doing archaeological research in Glen Canyon in 1957, as part of a team from the University of Utah—research required by federal law before the canyon was drowned by Lake Powell—the available topographic maps were derived from the maps made under the direction of A. H. Thompson during the Powell Expedition. They were accurate, useful maps.

12. For overall histories of the "Great Surveys" see Bartlett, *Great Surveys of the American West*, and Goetzmann, *Exploration and Empire*. For the King Survey and King's work with the California Geological Survey see Wilkins, *Clarence King*. For the work of Carleton E. Watkins with the California Geological Survey see Palmquist, *Carleton E. Watkins*, pp. 24–35, Alinder, *Carleton E. Watkins*, and Naef and Wood, *Era of Exploration*, pp. 79–90 and plates 1–34. For Timothy O'Sullivan's work with Mathew Brady and the King Survey see Horan, *Mathew Brady*, pp. 40–79, and Horan, *Timothy O'Sullivan*, pp. 27–214.

13. For Bell's and O'Sullivan's work with the Wheeler Survey see Horan, *Timothy O'Sullivan*, pp. 237–312, and Wheeler, *Photographs*. O'Sullivan's work has been assessed by Newhall and Newhall, *Timothy O'Sullivan*, Snyder, *American Frontiers*, Naef and Wood, *Era of Exploration*, pp. 125–36 and plates 35–64, and Dingus, *Photographic Artifacts of Timothy O'Sullivan*.

Between October 5 and 20, 1871, O'Sullivan, Lieutenant Wheeler, the geologist Grove Karl Gilbert, and others entered the lower end of the Grand Canyon by boat and struggled *upstream* against the current and the rapids as far as Diamond Creek. O'Sullivan took a number of photographs, only a few of which, unfortunately, survived. Technically, O'Sullivan's photographs were the first taken of the Grand Canyon, not those by Hillers or Fennemore, as the present author and others have maintained (Hillers, *Diary*, p. 13; Stegner, *Beyond the Hundredth Meridian*, p. 268).

14. W. H. Jackson's work for Hayden, as well as his remarkable career as a western photographer (he lived to be ninety-nine years old, dying in 1942) are well chronicled. See W. H. Jackson, *Diaries*, W. H. Jackson, *Pioneer Photographer*, W. H. Jackson, *Time Exposure*, C. S. Jackson, *Picture Maker of the Old West*, and Newhall and Edkins, *William H. Jackson*.

15. For overviews of western military expeditions and the artists who accompanied them, see Goetzmann, *Army Exploration*, and Wallace, *Great Reconnaissance*. For Peale and Seymour, see Ewers, *Artists of the Old West*, pp. 23–37. For the Kern brothers see Hine, *In the Shadow of Fremont*. For Möllhausen see Möllhausen, *Diary*.

16. Preuss, *Exploring with Fremont*, pp. 32–38.

17. For Carvalho see Sturhahn, *Carvalho*, pp. 94–98, and Rudisill, *Mirror Image*, pp. 101–2.

18. Simpson, *Report of Explorations*, pp. 8–9.

19. For Carvalho, Ives, and Simpson, see Taft, *Photography and the American Scene*, pp. 52, 266, and 290, note.

20. Many excellent surveys of photographic history are available. Here and in later chapters, information has been drawn from: Auer, *Illustrated History of the Camera*; Beaton and Buckland, *Magic Image*; Crawford, *Keepers of Light*; Darrah, *World of Stereographs*; Earle, *Points of View*; Gernsheim, *Origins of Photography*; Gilbert, *Photography: The Early Years*, pp. 1–36; Newhall, *Daguerreotype in America*; Newhall, *History of Photography*; Pollack, *Picture History of Photography*; Rinhart and Rinhart, *American Daguerreotype*; Rudisill, *Mirror Image*; Taft, *Photography and the American Scene*; and Welling, *Photography in America*.

21. The history of experiments in photographic chemistry is discussed by Gernsheim, *Origins of Photography*, passim, Taft, *Photography and the American Scene*, esp. pp. 102–34, and Crawford, *Keepers of Light*, passim.

22. For materials on stereo- and large-format cameras see Auer, *Illustrated History of the Camera*, Gilbert, *Photography: The Early Years*, Darrah, *World of Stereographs*, and Earle, *Points of View*. For equipment used by Hillers, Watkins, Weed, Muybridge, and Jackson see Hillers, *Diary*, fig. 1; Naef and Wood, *Era of Exploration*, pp. 54, 67, and figs. 68, 94; C. S. Jackson, *Picture Maker of the Old West*, pp. 223–29; and Taft, *Photography and the American Scene*, pp. 177–85.

23. Hillers, *Diary*, p. 24. In addition to Hillers's diary, see the diaries kept by others in the party in Gregory, Darrah, and Kelly, "Exploration of the Colorado River," passim. See also Fowler and Fowler, "John Wesley Powell's Journal," and Dellenbaugh, *Canyon Voyage*. Powell's own published version of the two river trips, written as if all events took place during the first, 1869, trip, is in his *Exploration of the Colorado River*.

24. Hillers, *Diary*, p. 23.

25. J. W. Powell, *Report on the Geology of the Uintah Mountains*.

26. With the exception of Hillers and Thompson, the other members of the 1871–72 river trips soon scattered. Almon Harris Thompson (1839–1906) remained Chief Topographer of the Powell Survey until 1879, when he became Chief Geographer of the U.S. Geological Survey, a position he held until his death. For his diary for the period 1872–75 see Thompson, "Diary." For biographical material on the other expedition members, see Gregory, Darrah, and Kelly, "Exploration of the Colorado River." For E. O. Beaman see note 30, below.

27. Hillers, *Diary*, passim.

28. F. S. Dellenbaugh to Robert Taft, Nov. 19, 1932, printed in Taft, *Photography and the American Scene*, pp. 289–90.

29. Hillers, *Diary*, pp. 81–82.

30. Hillers, *Diary*, p. 91. Beaman went to Salt Lake City, procured a pack horse outfit, and made a trip to the Hopi mesas in Arizona. (See Beaman, "Colorado Exploring Expedition," "Tour through the Grand Canon," "Among the Aztecs," and "Canons of the Colorado.") Subsequently, Beaman and Powell seem to have reached some sort of rapprochement. On Feb. 1, 1873, Beaman wrote to Powell from New York City offering to produce stereographs for him at $74 to $80 per thousand, an arrangement apparently not consummated. In February 1878 Beaman again wrote to Powell concerning their exchanging "sets of views," and offering to act as slide view operator if Powell planned to give lectures that year (Powell Survey Correspondence).

31. Taft, *Photography and the American Scene*, p. 290; Thompson, "Diary," p. 67; Hillers, *Diary*, p. 98.

32. A. H. Thompson to J. W. Powell, Mar. 11, 1872 (Powell Survey Correspondence).

33. Taft, *Photography and the American Scene*, p. 290.

34. J. K. Hillers to J. W. Powell, Apr. 25, 1872 (Powell Survey Correspondence).

35. The beauty of Glen Canyon is not well reflected in Fennemore's photographs. For modern photographs before the canyon was inundated by Lake Powell, see Eliot Porter, *The Place No One Knew*, and Porter's photographs in J. W. Powell, *Down the Colorado*.

36. A. H. Thompson to J. W. Powell, May 20, 1872 (Powell Survey Correspondence).

37. Thompson, "Diary," pp. 83–84.

38. Hillers, *Diary*, pp. 112–14.

39. Hillers, *Diary*, p. 128. O. C. and Seneca Howland, together with William Dunn, were the three who left the 1869 river trip at Separation Rapid in the Grand Canyon. They climbed out onto the Shivwits Plateau and were killed by Paiute Indians. In the summer of 1959, the present author spent four days in Music Temple making rubber latex molds of the names carved in the walls of the cavern, now under water. The molds are on deposit at the Museum of Natural History, University of Utah, Salt Lake City.

40. See Brooks, *John Doyle Lee*. The Powell Expedition visit is described on p. 312.

41. Hillers, *Diary*, pp. 129–31.

42. Darrah, "Beaman, Fennemore, Hillers," p. 492.

43. For an extensive discussion and analysis of Beaman's and Hillers's photographs of the Colorado River canyons see Stephens and Shoemaker, *In the Footsteps of John Wesley Powell*.

44. Hillers, *Diary*, p. 142.

45. W. C. Powell, "Journal," pp. 458–69, 479–90; Hillers, *Diary*, pp. 146–52; Jones diary in Gregory, Darrah, and Kelly, "Exploration of the Colorado River," p. 172; W. C. Powell, "Journal," pp. 465–66.

46. Kennard, *Hopi Kachinas*, p. 6. On photographers at Hopi, see for example Casagrande and Bourns, *Side Trips*, p. 100.

47. W. C. Powell, "Journal," p. 464.

48. Pyne, *Grove Karl Gilbert*, pp. 50, 57–95.

49. W. C. Powell, "Journal," p. 473.

50. According to Darrah, "Beaman, Fennemore, Hillers," p. 499, Dellenbaugh noted that the "blind box" was the portable photographic dark tent; "threedolite" was Hattan's name for the theodolite, and Steward was an "exhorter" because he swore like a trooper. The song is printed as the frontispiece of the published Powell Expedition diaries for 1871–72 (Gregory, Darrah, and Kelly, "Exploration of the Colorado River").

51. Thompson, "Diary," p. 108.

52. Wilmerding, "Luminist Movement," pp. 97–152. For discussions of Hillers's work see pp. 102, 139–40.

53. J. K. Hillers to J. W. Powell, May 25, 1873 (Powell Survey Correspondence).

54. Thompson, "Diary," passim.

Myself in the Water

Indians of the Canyon Country

While Hillers photographed the Zion Canyon and Wasatch Plateau regions and Thompson proceeded with the map making, Powell spent most of his time in Washington, D.C., during late 1872 and early 1873. In 1872 the Powells sold their home in Normal, Illinois, and moved to Washington—ultimately to a house at 910 M Street, N.W., where they would live until Powell's death in 1902. In later years, the rumor around the Powell Survey was that Powell paid off the mortgage on the M Street house from his share of receipts from the sales of Beaman's and Hillers's stereographs.

Powell was determined to carve out a career as a government scientist, using his Geological Survey as the vehicle. He had long-standing interests in both geology and American Indians. Now, as his work continued in the West, he expanded both those interests. During the winter of 1868–69, while he and Emma were camped in the White River valley of northwestern Colorado, Powell had begun studying the language and customs of a group of Ute Indians living nearby. He expanded his studies of the Ute-Southern Paiute language and its dialects as he continued his explorations in subsequent years. He also collected myths and tales and a range of other ethnographic data, as well as extensive collections of material culture.[1]

A significant part of Powell's anthropological program was to photograph the Indians of the Canyon Country. Beaman had made a number of good photographs of Indians in the Uintah Basin during the 1871 river trip. At Kanab, Utah, before Beaman and Powell had their falling out, Beaman had tried to photograph the Kaibab Southern Paiutes who were camped nearby. He

later wrote, however, that he was allowed to make only one photograph.[2]

In the fall of 1872 Powell again turned his attention to photographing the Kaibab Paiutes. By early October, they were back in their winter camp at the mouth of Upper Kanab Canyon, just above the Mormon settlement. The camp was occupied by members of Chuarumpeak's band, whose home territory centered on Kanab Creek and the Kaibab (or Buckskin, as the Mormons called it) Plateau to the south. The Kaibab people were among the last Indian groups in the American West to come into sustained contact with Euroamericans—Mormons, Mexicans, and "Mericats" (as the Indians called non-Mormon, non-Hispanic whites). The Kaibab, and other nearby Southern Paiute bands, had been preyed upon by Spanish, Mexican, Ute, and Navajo slave raiders for a century, since the opening of the Old Spanish Trail in the 1760s. Captured Paiutes were sold either in California or New Mexico. To escape their captors, the Kaibab and other bands had hidden in the remote areas of the Kaibab, Shivwits, and Wasatch plateaus. Jacob Hamblin, the Mormon explorer and missionary, founded Kanab, Utah, in 1869. By 1872 the Kaibab Indians who gathered around Kanab for part of the year had only just begun to acquire castoff whites' clothing and to use horses and guns.[3]

Hillers's diary has no entries for the dates, but Clem Powell recorded for October 4–5, 1872: "After breakfast Maj. [Powell], Jacob [Hamblin], Jack and I drove over to the Paute camp to picture it; were at [it] nearly all day. Braves, squaws, and pampooses were done up in the most artistic fashion, as also was the Ancient Arrow Maker. . . . Went over to the Indian camp to finish taking pictures. Took 5 or 6 negatives, one of the Arrow Maker

18. *A Tribal Council*, Kanab, Utah, October 4, 1872. John Wesley Powell (nearest camera) and Jacob Hamblin (on right) consulting with Chuarumpeak (rear center), leader of the Kaibab Paiute band. National Anthropological Archives, Smithsonian Institution.

19. *The Ta-vo-koki or Circle Dance (Winter Costume)*, Kanab, Utah, October 4, 1872. John Wesley Powell standing at left observing the dance, undoubtedly staged for the camera. National Anthropological Archives, Smithsonian Institution.

[fig. 20], one of them kindling fire and others."[4] Hamblin had considerable influence with the Indians, and undoubtedly he convinced them that no harm would come to them from the photography. Hillers's primary purpose was ethnographic documentation—to show the lifeways of the people. The set of photographs he made is one of the basic cultural records of Southern Paiute life in the early period of acculturation. While the pictures were obviously posed, they show the people in much more natural attitudes than the set of photographs Hillers made of them the following year. Chuarumpeak, the leader of the Kaibab Paiutes, is shown in Figure 18 consulting with Powell and Hamblin. By all accounts, he was a remarkable person. Powell used him as a guide and worked with him to quiet various Indian-white problems in southern Utah between 1870 and 1873. Powell later wrote about Chuarumpeak and his philosophical and perceptual insights.[5]

It was while Hillers was making his initial series of photographs of the Kaibab Paiutes in 1872 that the Indians gave him the name "Myself in the Water." The analogy was apt—the Indians could see themselves reflected in still water pools, just as they could see themselves reflected in Hillers's photographs. Indian people called other nineteenth-century photographers "Shadow Catcher" (Edward S. Curtis and David F. Berry among them)—also an apt name for a photographer. In later years Hillers would tell his son and daughter-in-law how he had been given his name by the Paiutes camped near Kanab, Utah, so many years before.[6]

By 1872–73 there had been a series of clashes in Utah and Nevada between white settlers and miners and the various Numic-speaking Indian groups. Reservations had been created for some bands and tribes, but the people wished to live their own lives and continue their annual subsistence rounds as they had for ages past. There were possibilities of more serious confrontations between Indians and whites. John Wesley Powell was keenly aware of the situation, and he grasped an opportunity to put his knowledge of the Numic peoples to use. He saw to it that his expertise came to the attention of the Bureau of Indian Affairs. In 1872 he was appointed Indian Commissioner for the tribes in southern Utah. Under this appointment, Thompson, sometimes aided by Hillers, spent a fair amount of time distributing goods to the Indians in and around Kanab and St. George, Utah. In early 1873 Powell's title was broadened to that of Special Commissioner of Indian Affairs. He and an Indian agent, George W. Ingalls, were assigned to investigate the "conditions and wants" of Indians of the Canyon Country and portions of the Great Basin. Their principal task was to locate reservations for Indians yet unsettled, and, in some cases, persuade other groups to remove to, and remain on, previously designated reservations. They proceeded with their task during the summer and fall of 1873.[7]

Ever alert to the value of publicity, Powell invited two men to come along with him for a portion of the trip, primarily to Zion and Grand Canyons. One was J. E. Colburn, a young New York Times reporter. The second was Thomas Moran, already famous as a landscape artist. In 1871 Moran had accompanied Powell's rival, F. V. Hayden, to the Yellowstone area to make sketches for Scribner's Monthly. It was during this trip that William Henry Jackson took his remarkable photographs of the wonders of Yellowstone that helped convince the Congress to set aside Yellowstone as the world's first national park. Moran was inspired to paint his magnificent seven-by-twelve-foot Grand Canyon of the Yellowstone after he returned. The U.S. Congress paid him $10,000 for the painting and ordered it hung in the Senate lobby of the Capitol.[8]

Powell was well aware of Moran's work and had invited him to join the 1872 trip into the Grand Canyon, but Moran had not been able to come along. Powell left the invitation open, and on July 6, 1873, Moran and Colburn met him and Ingalls in Salt Lake City. The party called on Brigham Young and other Mormon leaders, as was customary for all prominent visitors to Utah at the time. Given the tensions during the nineteenth century between Mormons and non-Mormons, a courtesy visit informed the Mormon leadership of the activities of the visitors and usually secured the cooperation of the citizenry throughout the territory. After the visit the four started southward through central Utah. Powell and Ingalls had to stop at various Indian encampments to conduct their investigations and meetings. Moran and Colburn went on and met one of Powell's men, George Adair, at Sheep Troughs, near Short Creek (now Colorado

20. *The Arrow Maker and His Daughter*, Kanab, Utah, October 4-5, 1872. The man is sitting outside his wickiup with two young children. He is holding a hafted stone knife, not an arrow. The knife, and many of the other material culture items visible in the October 1872 photographs, are part of the Powell collection now in the National Museum of Natural History. National Anthropological Archives, Smithsonian Institution.

City), Arizona, on July 30, 1873. Adair guided them to Zion Canyon. Hillers and Thompson then arrived and guided the two men along the south rim of Parunuweap Canyon, overlooking the Kolob Plateau and Zion Canyon. Moran was fascinated by the country, a fascination later expressed in several paintings and engravings of the Virgin River valley.[9]

On August 4, 1873, as Colburn wrote, "Mr. Moran, Mr. John K. Hillers, the photographer of the Powell expedition, and myself with a Mr. [Nathan] Adams, a resident of Kanab, for cook and 'packer' and a Pi Ute Indian, whom we called Jim," started on horseback for Mt. Trumbull on the North Rim of the Grand Canyon, with "two pack mules, one for Mr. Hillers' photographic apparatus, and the other for our blankets and rations for ten days." The party spent two days "at the foot of To-ro-weap. Hillers and Moran made several photographs and sketches." Moran later wrote to his wife that while the party was at Toroweap, "Hillers . . . was bringing a canteen of water from [a water hole] when a huge rattlesnake glided between his feet and he got a thorough scare . . . I killed it with a stone. It measured nearly 3½ feet long . . . on our trip to the Virgin River Jack had another narrow escape from a rattlesnake. He was talking to me and had both his elbows right over a rattler which Colburn shot."[10]

Hillers and Powell wanted to make some additional photographs of Chuarumpeak's band, especially stereographs. In 1868, during his winter with the White River Utes in northwestern Colorado, Powell had collected a number of items of clothing; he possibly collected others in 1870 and 1871. These had been placed in the museum collection at Illinois Normal University. (They would later find their way into the Smithsonian collections.) Now in 1873 Powell brought some of the garments to southern Utah, to dress up the Kaibab Paiutes. The previous year Powell's sister, Ellen Thompson, had directed the Indians in the manufacture of various "Indian" clothing items, as well as feathered headdresses. These apparently were stored with someone at Marysvale, Utah, after A. H. Thompson had left the Gunnison area and returned to Kanab. Thompson telegraphed Powell to have the "trunk of Indian clothing" sent back to Kanab. Powell and James C. Pilling, his chief clerk, arrived with the clothing in Kanab on August 11.[11]

Hillers and Moran arrived back from Mt. Trumbull and prepared to photograph Chuarumpeak and his band.

They were first decked out in the Ute clothing and the headdresses and fringed buckskin shirts previously made under Ellen Thompson's direction. Hillers says he enlisted Moran to pose the Indians in "effective attitudes" (figs. 22, 23). These rather affected effective attitudes mimic poses commonly used by nineteenth-century portrait photographers. The Indian people look thoroughly uncomfortable in most of the photographs. Hillers posed Moran and Colburn with a young Paiute boy, making at least two variant shots of the trio (e.g., fig. 21). According to a note on the back of Moran's copy of one of the photographs, the boy's father offered to sell the boy to Moran; "Mr. Moran was tempted. He liked the boy."[12]

21. J. E. Colburn (left), Thomas Moran (right), and Kaibab Paiute boy, August 13, 1873. National Anthropological Archives, Smithsonian Institution.

22. *Group of Indians in Native Dress,* Kanab, Utah, August 12-13, 1873. Kaibab Paiutes dressed in fake headdresses. National Anthropological Archives, Smithsonian Institution.

The photographs Hillers had made in the fall of 1872 were primarily ethnographic documents. Those made with Moran's advice in 1873 were for the stereograph trade. A few of the photographs, both those made at Kanab and those made in the following weeks in the Moapa Valley, are slightly titillating; some women were posed with one or both breasts exposed. Hillers had discovered what many other nineteenth-century photographers knew about the Victorian world: suggestive photographs of bare-breasted women were acceptable and could be published as long as the women were non-white "natives."[13]

On August 14, 1873, Powell, Hillers, Moran, Colburn, Pilling, and others set out for the Kaibab Plateau. They were soon joined by George Ingalls. There Hillers caught the party in repose (fig. 24). Moran was deeply moved by the Grand Canyon. After his return to the East, he made illustrations for various magazines using Grand Canyon themes. He illustrated Powell's 1875 articles in *Scribner's Monthly* on the Canyon Country, using Hillers's photographs as the basis for several of the illustrations.[14] He also produced another majestic painting, *The Chasm of the Colorado*. It too was purchased by the U.S. Congress for $10,000 and hung for many years in the Senate lobby of the Capitol, along with the *Grand Canyon of the Yellowstone*.[15] In later years Moran returned often to the Grand Canyon and produced a number of other paintings and watercolors of it.

Following the Kaibab Plateau trip, Moran and Colburn returned to New York. Powell, Ingalls, and Hillers traveled to St. George, Utah, and thence to Moapa and Las Vegas, Nevada, to continue Powell's duties as Special Indian Commissioner. Of particular importance was a meeting of several Southern Paiute bands with Powell and Ingalls, along with a number of local Mormon leaders and a few non-Mormon whites, near St. George in September 1873 (fig. 25). From St. George, the party went on to the Moapa Valley and Las Vegas, Nevada. In 1873 Las Vegas was a small Mormon way station on the Old Spanish Trail route to southern California. Bands of Southern Paiutes congregated around the vegas, the meadows watered by artesian springs. The area is adjacent to present-day downtown Las Vegas. Hillers made a number of portraits at both Moapa and Las Vegas (e.g., figs. 26–28). *The Old Gamblers* (fig. 28) demonstrates that Las Vegas has a longer history of gaming than the present-day Chamber of Commerce realizes.

23. *The Empty Cradle*. Kaibab Paiute woman, Kanab, Utah, August 13, 1873. This photograph became the subject of a Thomas Moran etching of the same name. Henry E. Huntington Library and Art Gallery.

24. Powell party on Kaibab Plateau, August 1873. Seated, left to right: James C. Pilling, John Wesley Powell, "Jim," a Kaibab Paiute, Thomas Moran, J. E. Colburn, George W. Ingalls. Standing, Nathan Adams. Henry E. Huntington Library and Art Gallery.

25. Southern Paiute Indians and Mormons meeting with J. W. Powell and G. Ingalls, outside St. George, Utah, September 1873. Powell standing at left, Ingalls seated at Powell's feet, Chuarumpeak (in beaded shirt) standing at right center. National Anthropological Archives, Smithsonian Institution.

26. *Kaiar, in Calico Dress,* Las Vegas, Nevada, September 1873. National Anthropological Archives, Smithsonian Institution.

27. *Antinaints, Putusive and Wichuts,* Las Vegas, Nevada, September 1873. National Anthropological Archives, Smithsonian Institution.

the desired information, but said he had little advice to offer. You are a clean worker in which lies the great secret of Photography [Watkins said]. He then showed me the manipulations of the Camera and Developing dishes. Next day I returned to the Gallery but found Mr. Watkins busily engaged in packing up his "traps" for a trip to Weber Canon, Utah, perhaps you saw him, he intended to visit Salt Lake City. I hope you will get out your book or rather have it printed to your entire satisfaction. I perhaps am a little enthusiastic when I say that I could sell 200 copies myself. The Photographs will sell like hot cakes I have not the least doubt.

How is the little Snow Flake [the Powells' daughter, Mary]? Should I not come to Washington please send me a copy of that "crooked toe" [?] Give my regards to Mrs. Powell, Mr. [James C.] Pilling the "positive man" also Colburn and Moran. By the way how is our "Grand Canyon of the Colorado" Picture [Moran's painting] progressing? . . . I have money enough to last but should you wish to dispence with my service altogether please let me know in your next, so that I may be able to look out for "Breakers" ahead. I hate to part from the old ship but if circumstances are such I will have to lay by with a long line and keep her in sight. I like to know where old Harry Thompson is, give him my best wishes.
I am ever thine,
Jack[16]

Back on the "Old Ship"

In early 1874, Powell embarked on an extensive lecture tour in the East and Middle West. He sent for Hillers, who accompanied him as projectionist of the "views" of the Canyon Country and its native inhabitants. A. H. Thompson "saw Major and Jack" on February 22, 1874, in Chicago during the lecture tour.[17] Powell was able to secure additional appropriations for his survey, and Hillers returned to the payroll in the summer of 1874, probably after the beginning of the federal fiscal year.

Powell planned a trip to the upper Green River and the Uintah Basin for the late summer and early fall of 1874. He took Hillers and Pilling with him. Details of this trip are sketchy (there are no known diaries from the

Hard Times

After completing the survey of the Indians, Powell returned to Washington, D.C., to write his report, and to lobby for continued support for his survey. But the financial panic of 1873 had hit hard, and Powell was able to obtain only $10,000 for the fiscal year 1873–74, not enough to keep everyone going. Hillers agreed to go on furlough until more funds could be obtained. He returned to San Francisco to stay with his brother Richard. From there he wrote Powell in December 1873:

Dear Major,

This morning I received your letter containing two orders for $50. each. I would have written to you before but I waited for a note from you according to agreement. I have enjoyed but poor health since my arrival here. The sudden change no doubt has been the cause. It has been raining off and on ever since my arrival.

I presented my letter to Mr. [Carleton] Watkins who received me very kindly. Showed him my work which he pronounced excellent. Told me that he was willing to give me all trip), but apparently the trio traveled by horseback and pack train in the Uintah Basin and through the Uintah Mountains on the north side of the basin. Powell continued his study of the geology of the region. Hillers took photographs during the trip, but only a few can be attributed to him with certainty (e.g., figs. 29–32).[18]

When Powell, Pilling, and Hillers returned to Washington in the fall of 1874, Hillers was able to settle in for the first time to do some extensive and sustained darkroom work. He also had to find a place to live. Hillers's name does not appear in District of Columbia directories until 1876, when he is listed as "photo. Powell's Exped. 910 M. St." The address is Powell's house; the same listing is given for 1877. It is not known whether Hillers actually lived with the Powells, or whether he lived elsewhere and used Powell's address for mail.[19]

Part of Hillers's job was to supervise the production of the various sets of stereopticon "views," or "stereographs." Stereo cameras produced dual images of one scene. When mounted on a card at the proper spacing and viewed through the lenses of a stereoscope, a three-dimensional effect was produced. By 1874, stereographs had entranced people around the world. Oliver Wendell Holmes had coined the term "stereograph" some years earlier. Stereoscopic daguerreotypes were produced as early as 1849; stereoscopic photographs were shown at the Crystal Palace Exhibition in London in 1851. They created a sensation, and their appearance marked the beginnings of the fad of stereoscopy that would last until 1914, and in some forms to the present day. In 1856 the English essayist Robert Hunt wrote, "The stereoscope is now seen in every drawing room; philosophers talk learnedly upon it, ladies are delighted with its magical representations and children play with it." By 1874 stereographs were produced in many parts of the world by the hundreds of thousands yearly.[20]

Stereographs of western scenes were sold as early as 1858. For example, Charles L. Weed, Eadweard Muybridge, and Carleton E. Watkins produced stereographs of California scenes, especially of Yosemite Valley, throughout the 1860s. All the photographers who worked for the Great Surveys made stereographs, particularly W. H. Jackson, since his income depended, in part, on their sales. Jackson held full rights to his negatives, and sold many sets of prints from the more than 2,200 negatives he produced. O'Sullivan made some stereographs when he worked for Clarence King, but relatively few

were distributed and apparently none were sold commercially. O'Sullivan and William Bell did, however, produce about 700 stereographs for the Wheeler Survey between 1871 and 1875.

For the Powell Survey, Beaman, Fennemore, and Hillers produced about 1,400 stereographs, of which about 650 were sold commercially in sets as well as being distributed to Congressmen and other influential people. The correspondence files of the Powell Survey for much of the 1870s contain copies of numerous letters that accompanied photographic "small tokens of esteem," which Powell annually distributed around the time of Congressional appropriations hearings. Proceeds from the sale of stereographs made by Hillers were split forty percent to Powell and thirty percent each to Thompson and Hillers. Powell kept the proceeds from the sale of those stereographs made by Beaman and the relatively few made by Fennemore. In addition, Hillers received a salary of around $1,200 per year.[21]

By the end of 1874, both Powell and Hillers had weathered financial "breakers," and their ship was about to head in new directions. Hillers was becoming known for his photographs, both through the sales of stereographs and through his large-format prints of the wonders and native peoples of the Canyon Country. An example of his notoriety is seen in a review of Hillers's photographs of the Southern Paiutes that appeared in 1874 in the *New York Graphic:* "The redskins exhibit delicate limbs, small hands and feet, and are finely sculptured in what the French call attachments—that is, the ankles and wrists. Some of the old men . . . with wrinkled visages, scraggly beards and horned caps made of antelope heads [fig. 27] look like melodramatic sorcerers. . . . The young matrons and maids [figs. 19, 26] . . . are primitive goddesses."[22] It is unlikely that the Paiutes of Utah and Nevada, who were struggling to maintain their traditional lifeways, thought of themselves in such terms.

Finally, in addition to achieving some fame, Hillers also was at last able to put down roots. Between 1874 and 1879 he lived in Washington for usually half the year, more or less. The rest of the time was spent in the field, doing photography as Powell directed and helping with the logistics of wagons and pack mules used in support of the survey field parties.

29. Head of Ladore Canyon, Green River, Wyoming, Fall 1874. James C. Pilling seated in foreground, just inside the Gate of Ladore, as Powell named the head of the canyon. National Archives, Geological Survey Collection.

30. *The Mirror Case*, Uintah Valley, Utah, Fall 1874. Major Powell and Tau-ruv, a Ute Indian woman, probably at or near the Uintah Ute Indian Agency. National Anthropological Archives, Smithsonian Institution.

31. *Pah-ri-ats, in Native Winter Dress,* Uintah Valley, Utah, Fall 1874. Powell used a woodcut from this photograph as an illustration in his *Exploration of the Colorado River* monograph in 1875. National Anthropological Archives, Smithsonian Institution.

32. *Antero, War Chief of the Uintah Utes,* Uintah Valley, Utah, Fall 1874. Antero played a prominent part in the so-called "Black Hawk War," a bitterly fought series of altercations between various Utes and Mormon settlers in Utah between 1865 and 1872. At the conclusion of hostilities, Antero and other Ute leaders were taken to Washington, D.C., to meet President Ulysses S. Grant and voice their grievances, but to little avail. National Anthropological Archives, Smithsonian Institution.

Notes

1. Powell collected large quantities of ethnographic and linguistic data on, as well as making extensive material culture collections from, the various Numic groups in the Canyon Country and the Great Basin between 1868 and 1880. He intended to write a comprehensive report on these materials, but never did. The present author and his colleagues finally undertook the task on Powell's behalf a century later. See Fowler and Fowler, *Anthropology of the Numa,* Fowler and Matley, *Material Culture of the Numa,* and Fowler, Euler, and Fowler, *Powell and the Anthropology of the Canyon Country.*

2. Beaman, "Canons of the Colorado," p. 547. The photograph is possibly BAE# 1593–c, attributed to Hillers, 1873, in the National Anthropological Archives, Smithsonian Institution.

3. The impact of slave raiding on various Numic peoples is discussed by Malouf and Malouf, "Effects of Spanish Slavery." For Jacob Hamblin see Bailey, *Jacob Hamblin.*

4. W. C. Powell, "Journal," p. 457.

5. Powell discusses Chuarumpeak in J. W. Powell, "Chuar's Illusion."

6. Mrs. Lila Hillers, personal communication, May 1968, Washington, D.C.

7. Fowler and Fowler, *Anthropology of the Numa,* pp. 97–119.

8. Wilkins, *Thomas Moran,* pp. 57–71. See also Braff, *Thomas Moran,* and Lindstrom, *Moran in Utah.*

9. Wilkins, *Thomas Moran,* p. 77; Colburn, "Land of Mormon," p. 2; Colburn, "Colorado Canyon," p. 2. Thompson, "Diary," p. 114 gives the date as July 30, 1873.

10. Colburn, "Land of Mormon," p. 2; Bassford and Fryxell, *Home-Thoughts from Afar,* p. 40.

11. Thompson, "Diary," p. 114.

12. Wilkins, *Thomas Moran,* pp. 82–83. The photograph is in the Moran Collection at the East Hampton, New York, Free Library.

13. For additional discussion and ethnographic analyses of Hillers's Numa photographs see Hillers, *Diary,* figs. 14–22, and various figures in Fowler and Fowler, *Anthropology of the Numa,* and Fowler and Matley, *Material Culture of the Numa.* See also Steward, *Notes on Hillers' Photographs,* and Euler, *Southern Paiute Ethnohistory,* appendix I.

14. J. W. Powell, "Canons of the Colorado," "Overland Trip to the Grand Canon," and "Ancient Province of Tusayan."

15. Wilkins, *Thomas Moran,* p. 93.

16. J. K. Hillers to J. W. Powell, Dec. 15, 1873 (Powell Survey Correspondence). By the time of Hillers's visit, Watkins was nationally known for his work, especially his magnificent photographs of Yosemite Valley. Praise from Watkins was high praise indeed! Watkins, and William Keath, a landscape painter, did, as Hillers says, travel to Weber Canyon and Salt Lake City, during late November and early December 1873. Watkins made numerous photographs and stereographs during the trip (Palmquist, *Carleton E. Watkins,* pp. 48–49).

17. Thompson, "Diary," p. 120.

18. J. W. Powell, *Exploration of the Colorado River,* p. 10. The attribution problems regarding Hillers's 1874 photographs are discussed in the appendix to the present volume.

19. Hillers is not listed in District of Columbia directories for 1878. For 1879, he is listed as "photographer" at 607 7th St., N.W. For 1880 and 1881 his address is listed as 714 N St., N.W.; for 1882 and 1883 at 1011 7th St., N.W. I am indebted to Paula Richardson Fleming of the National Anthropological Archives, Smithsonian Institution, for this information.

20. The discussion of the history of stereographs is drawn from Auer, *Illustrated History of the Camera,* pp. 224–41, Darrah, *World of Stereographs,* and Earle, *Points of View.* On Oliver Wendell Holmes see his "Stereoscope and Stereography" and "Doings of the Sunbeam." The Robert Hunt quotation is from the *Art Journal,* March 1856, cited by Earle, *Points of View,* p. 18.

21. Hillers, *Diary,* pp. 7–8; Darrah, *World of Stereographs,* pp. 85–93.

22. Cited in Wilkins, *Thomas Moran,* pp. 82–83.

Indian Territory and the 1876 Centennial Exhibition

A Grand Celebration

As the year 1876 approached, the people of the United States prepared for a centennial celebration of the Declaration of Independence and subsequent nationhood. In a century the United States had gone from Thomas Jefferson's nation of small farmers to a major industrial power. The country had survived the rending trauma of the Civil War. Now all faces were turned westward, or toward Progress, or both, however these were conceived. The country was still expanding, still being settled. Some areas were still being explored by Euroamericans, who were seeing for the first time land that Native Americans had known for millennia.

The people of the United States decided to celebrate their first century of independence and progress by holding a great exhibition—one to rival, if not surpass, those held periodically since 1851 in London, Paris, Vienna, and New York City.[1] This extravaganza would clearly demonstrate to the world that the United States had come of age, commercially, industrially, and culturally. The exhibition, fittingly, was to be held in Philadelphia, where the Declaration of Independence had been signed, although many other cities were eager to host the affair and reap the anticipated profits.

Many exhibit halls were planned, including a federal Government Building. The Smithsonian Institution, in the person of its energetic Assistant Secretary, Spencer F. Baird, was assigned a key role in developing the government exhibits. Four government agencies proposed exhibits relating to American Indian ethnography or archaeology, the Bureau of Indian Affairs, the Smithsonian, and both the Powell and the Hayden surveys. In 1875–76

Powell and Hayden were administratively under the Department of the Interior; they were hotly competing for public recognition and continued Congressional support. Both men planned to make extensive use of photographs.

Indian Territory

Powell and Spencer Baird concluded that the Indian photographic exhibits should include portraits and scenes of life in Indian Territory—the great unfenced prison where Indians had been (and were being) herded out of the way of white settlement and development. Powell sent Hillers to Oklahoma on the first of May, 1875. On May 4 Hillers met George Ingalls in St. Louis. Ingalls had gone on from his 1873 assignment with Powell to be a special agent of the Bureau of Indian Affairs in Indian Territory.

The two continued on to Muskogee (map 2). There Hillers rented a wagon to carry his "traps" to Okmulgee, the capital of the Creek Nation since 1867. Beginning in 1870, the Bureau of Indian Affairs had annually convened a General Council of the Indian Territory at Okmulgee. The Council was supposed to represent all the nations and tribes in the Territory.[2]

When Hillers arrived in Okmulgee, he found the Council already in session. Some of the delegates, especially the Cheyennes, Arapahoes, and Pawnees, were new arrivals, only recently resettled in Indian Territory, after being driven from their traditional territories in the central and northern Plains. Others, such as the "Five Civilized Tribes"—Cherokee, Choctaw, Seminole, Creek, and Chickasaw—had been settled in Indian Territory for nearly forty years.

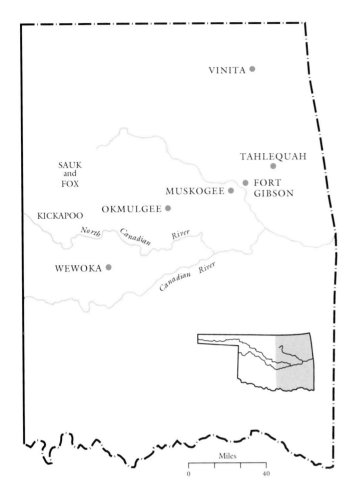

MAP 2. Eastern Indian Territory (Oklahoma).

Members of the Five Tribes had suffered through the tragic and inhumane Indian Removal of the 1830s and 1840s, forced from their homelands in the Southeast.[3] By 1875 the survivors and their descendants were well established, had strong tribal governments, and gained their livelihoods through farming and commerce. Thus Hillers found both old and new arrivals at Okmulgee, and as he moved around the Territory he was able to see, meet, and photograph the well-acculturated members of the Five Tribes, as well as the newcomers from the High Plains.

Hillers made two sets of photographs in Indian Territory. One set he took back to Washington for use in the Philadelphia exhibit, although few were apparently used. The second set he gave to George Ingalls. The latter includes portraits of members of the Five Tribes and pictures of buildings and natural landmarks.[4] The photographs used at Philadelphia were of "wild" Indians, at

least what the American public of 1876 thought of as wild, for example members of those tribes that attended General George Custer's last display of hubris at the Little Big Horn a few weeks after the Centennial Exhibition opened far away in Philadelphia. The photographs Hillers gave to Ingalls were of men in frock coats and women in bustled dresses, both living in well-built brick houses—clearly not the sort of Indians the public at Philadelphia expected to see.

Hillers began taking photographs in Okmulgee on May 9, 1875, with a shot of F. B. Severs Cash Store (fig. 33). The following five days were very busy ones, "making pictures of Indians." As Hillers wrote to brother Richard, "I found six Cheyennes who had just left the war path, all strappen big fellows. I took them among the rocks and set them up as food for my camera. I stripped them to the buff, not even a stitch on them except for a breach clout, and succeeded in making pictures of them all."[5] In addition to the Cheyenne, Hillers also made portraits of prominent Pawnee and Arapaho leaders (figs. 34–36).

On May 13, Hillers photographed the General Council (fig. 37). Among those in the photograph are George W. Ingalls and General John Peter Cleaver Shanks. General Shanks was a Special Commissioner for the Bureau of Indian Affairs who had addressed the Council on May 5.[6]

After finishing at Okmulgee, Hillers headed southwest to Wewoka, the capital of the Seminole Nation. He was accompanied on the trip by John F. Brown, known as Governor Brown. Brown was a partner in a highly successful business, the Wewoka Trading Company. He was the son of a Scottish physician, Dr. John Frippo Brown, and a Seminole mother. Dr. Brown had been with the Seminoles during their move to Indian Territory from Florida.[7] Along the way, Hillers photographed "two little cascades" (figs. 38, 39). East of Wewoka he "found the river up and booming. Crossed on a large sycamore which had been felled across the stream." The "crossing" was apparently for photographic purposes (fig. 40), because Hillers was driving a spring wagon drawn by a pair of mules.

Arriving in Wewoka, Hillers again met Ingalls and General Shanks. They had come to Wewoka to accompany a group of Cheyennes back to the Cheyenne-Arapaho reservation in western Indian Territory.[8] With the Cheyennes was Philip McCusker, a white married to a Comanche woman and regarded as the official interpreter for the Comanche tribe. Hillers took photographs at the

33. F. B. Severs Cash Store,
Okmulgee, Indian Territory,
May 9, 1875. Henry E. Hunt-
ington Library and Art
Gallery.

Cheyenne camp on May 18, before the start of the west-ward trip (figs. 41, 42).

The following day Hillers traveled fifteen miles to visit Colonel John Jumper, the chief of the Seminole Nation. Jumper had been a leader of a faction sympathetic to the Confederacy in the Civil War and had organized and led the Seminole Battalion in the Confederate army. Hillers wrote of him, "I went to the home of that re-nown[ed] chieftain, old John Jumper, who ten years ago counted his scalps by the hundred, and who then wore a buckskin shirt trimmed with the hair of his victims, but now a peaceable farmer and expounder of the Gospel. Liken to Paul, he had seen a vision, buried the tomahawk

and drove the scalping knife into a large sycamore. . . . He formerly was a poligamist and had three wives, but when he joined the church he was told to let two of them go and retain only one. He kept the children. What became of the women I could not learn."9 While visiting Jumper, Hillers also photographed "John Jumper's church" (fig. 43), and a dog trot cabin listed in Ingalls's catalog as "Residence of Sec[retary] of Seminole Tribe" (fig. 44).

Returning to Wewoka, Hillers photographed John F. Brown and his family on May 20 (fig. 45). He then turned eastward to Tahlequah, via Okmulgee, Muskogee, and Fort Gibson. He arrived in Tahlequah, the capital of

34. Lone Chief, Pawnee. Okmulgee, Indian Territory, May 14, 1875. Lone Chief was a ritual and political leader of one of the four main Skidi Pawnee villages, Tuwahukasa, or "Village-across-a-ridge." Traditional Skidi Pawnee territory was in Nebraska, centered near present-day Genoa. Lone Chief and other tribal leaders led their people to Indian Territory between 1870 and 1875 to join their linguistic relatives, the Wichita. (See Weltfish, *The Lost Universe*, pp. 4-5, 86.) Henry E. Huntington Library and Art Gallery.

35. Yellow Bear and his wife, Arapahoes. Okmulgee, Indian Territory, May 11 or 12, 1875. Yellow Bear was a leader of a Southern Arapaho band. During the 1860s he participated in numerous battles that the Arapaho and the Cheyenne fought against the U.S. Army. In 1869 he led his people to the Cheyenne-Arapaho reservation in Indian Territory. The following year, because of his efforts to establish peaceful relations among the tribes and with the whites, he was awarded a Peace Medal, which he is wearing in the photograph. By 1873, Yellow Bear was regarded as a principal chief of the Medicine Lodge Council. Later he was a leader in attempting to turn his people away from hunting and toward ranching as a means of livelihood, and was himself a successful rancher. (See Trenholm, *The Arapahoes*, pp. 229-46, 267.) Henry E. Huntington Library and Art Gallery.

STARVING ELK

36. Mok-ta-vo-ints, or Starving Elk, Cheyenne. Okmulgee, Indian Territory, May 10, 1875. Starving Elk was a prominent Northern Cheyenne warrior. He participated in the Beecher Island fight in 1868, when a combined force of Sioux, Arapahoes, and Cheyennes fought against Major George A. Forsyth and a detachment of white military scouts. In 1879-80 he was part of the Northern Cheyennes' epic march, led by Little Wolf and Dull Knife, from the detested Indian Territory back to their beloved Wyoming-Montana homelands. The march ended with their surrender and internment at Fort Keogh, Montana Territory. There Starving Elk was killed by Little Wolf in a quarrel over the latter's wife. (See Grinnell, *The Fighting Cheyennes*, pp. 277-92, 398-413.) National Anthropological Archives, Smithsonian Institution.

37. General Council of Indian Tribes at Okmulgee, Indian Territory, May 13, 1875. G. W. Ingalls seated second from left; General John Peter Cleaver Shanks seated left center. Henry E. Huntington Library and Art Gallery.

38. Limestone Creek, Indian Territory, May 15 or 16, 1875. Henry E. Huntington Library and Art Gallery.

39. Salt Creek Rapids, Indian Territory, May 15 or 16, 1875. Henry E. Huntington Library and Art Gallery.

40. *Crossing Stream on Large Fallen Sycamore,* near Wewoka, Indian Territory, May 16, 1875. John F. Brown on left; General J. P. C. Shanks on right. The boy in the center is unidentified. Shanks was on his way to Wewoka and must have caught up to Hillers at the crossing. Henry E. Huntington Library and Art Gallery.

41. Cheyenne encampment at Wewoka, Indian Territory, May 18, 1875. Philip McCusker and his wife at left. Henry E. Huntington Library and Art Gallery.

the Cherokee Nation, on May 26. There he lodged with the Reverend John Buttrick Jones, a Baptist missionary who had been an Indian agent to the Cherokees in 1872–73. According to Ingalls's catalog, "Rev. J. B. Jones and family [were] adopted by [Cherokee] council [as] members of Tribe." The next morning Hillers "made pictures of [Jones's] house and family and three young half-breeds" (figs. 46, 47). He also made a portrait of Jones's daughter Mary (fig. 48), listed by Ingalls as "Flower Girl, an adopted White by act of Council."

On May 28, Hillers, accompanied by "Mr. Stevens and Williams . . . [and] Gus went to Hildebrand Falls" (fig. 49).[10] Presumably Stevens, Williams, and Gus are among those at the top of the falls in the photograph. The following day Hillers photographed various buildings in Tahlequah, including the Cherokee Nation council house, said to have cost $22,000 to construct (fig. 50). He also took photographs at the Ladies' Seminary. His diary reads, "Made pictures of all the pupils. Quite a lot of pretty girls." The entry for the following day, Sunday, May 30, says, "Fasted."[11] But in a letter to his brother Richard, Hillers tells quite another story.

Hillers wrote that he was smitten by one of the young ladies at the Seminary. She had a "beautiful form such as few women possess . . . large lustrous black eyes and long jet black hair. . . . Her regular cut features, and a smile so captivating threw me almost into Cupid's arms, and for a moment I forgot my bachelor's resolution." Hillers posed this charming "Vision" and made her photograph. "I made the picture which was truly a good one, and how it happened I could not tell, for my nerves were all unstrung, my hand trembling, I could scarcely handle the plate."

Pining for his "Ideal," Hillers "mounted my horse and sadly rode away." But the "Ideal," Alvoretta Jerome, contrived to leave the Seminary, catch up with Hillers, and take him to her home. There he met her parents, sang duets with her ("What are the Wild Waves Saying"), and stayed overnight as a house guest. The next day, Hillers and Alvoretta started out to visit a cascade near the Jerome house. "The Colonel [her father], feeling somewhat indisposed, excused himself, so I had my queen for a companion and guide. The road to the cascade led through an oak grove . . ." There the letter ends.[12] No photograph of the charming young woman exists in known collections of Hillers's photographs. Perhaps he kept it; perhaps he gave it to Ms. Jerome. Whatever the outcome of the *tête-*

42. Opposite top: Cheyenne encampment at Wewoka, Indian Territory, May 18, 1875. Philip McCusker standing, right center; G. W. Ingalls seated, holding cradleboard. Henry E. Huntington Library and Art Gallery.

43. Opposite bottom: *John Jumper's Church,* near Wewoka, Indian Territory, May 19, 1875. Henry E. Huntington Library and Art Gallery.

44. Left: *Residence of Secretary of Seminole Tribe,* near Wewoka, Indian Territory, May 19, 1875. Henry E. Huntington Library and Art Gallery.

45. Below: John F. Brown and family, Wewoka, Indian Territory, May 20, 1875. Henry E. Huntington Library and Art Gallery.

46. Reverend John Buttrick Jones and family, Tahlequah, Indian Territory, May 27, 1875. Henry E. Huntington Library and Art Gallery.

47. Reverend John Buttrick Jones's house and family, Tahlequah, Indian Territory, May 27, 1875. Henry E. Huntington Library and Art Gallery.

48. Mary Jones, daughter of
J. B. Jones, Tahlequah, Indian
Territory, May 27, 1875. Henry
E. Huntington Library and
Art Gallery.

49. Hildebrand Falls, Indian
Territory, May 28, 1875. Henry
E. Huntington Library and
Art Gallery.

50. Cherokee Council House,
Tahlequah, Indian Territory,
May 29, 1875. Henry E.
Huntington Library and
Art Gallery.

51. William Potter Ross,
Cherokee leader, Fort Gibson,
Indian Territory, June 1, 1875.
Henry E. Huntington Library
and Art Gallery.

à-tête, Hillers remained a bachelor another eight years.

If his diary chronology is accurate, on the day after the trip to the falls Hillers traveled to Fort Gibson, where he photographed William Potter Ross (fig. 51). Ross was elected principal chief of the Cherokees in 1866–67 and again in 1872–75. He was the nephew of Chief John Ross who led the Cherokee Nation from 1828 to 1866.[13] Subsequently Hillers traveled to the Sac and Fox agency and then to the Kickapoo towns, making a number of photographs.

Return to Utah

Hillers's diary ends on June 10, 1875. He presumably returned to Washington, D.C., soon thereafter, and then headed west again. By early July he was back in southern Utah, where he joined A. H. Thompson, the geologist Grove Karl Gilbert, and their party. A brilliant geologist, Gilbert had been with the Wheeler Survey, but he was too good a scientist and too constrained by military organization and procedures to remain. He joined Powell's survey in November 1874. In the summer of 1875 Gilbert was about to begin his study of the Henry Mountains. The Henrys were the last mountains in the contiguous forty-eight states to be discovered and named. Powell had named them in 1869 for Joseph Henry, first Secretary of the Smithsonian Institution. Gilbert came to understand their structure, calling them "laccoliths" (that is, domes of interleaved layers of sedimentary rocks and lava sheets pushed up by great masses of lava), a then-new concept in geology.[14]

Hillers, Gilbert, Thompson, and W. H. Graves, a geological assistant, traversed the Aquarius Plateau, partially retracing the route taken by Thompson, Hillers, and others in 1872. On the Aquarius (or Boulder Mountain, as it is locally known), Hillers photographed several of the small lakes (figs. 52, 53). During the trip, one of the party, probably Gilbert or Thompson, photographed Hillers (fig. 54).

From Tantalus Valley, at the foot of the Henry Mountains, the party retraced its steps across the Aquarius Plateau, turning south to descend onto, and

52. Unnamed lake, Aquarius Plateau, southern Utah, July 1875. National Archives photo no. 57-PS-448 (Geological Survey Collection).

74

53. Winslow Creek, Aquarius Plateau, southern Utah, July 1875. Winslow Creek is a tributary of the Escalante River. In 1965 the National Board of Geographic Names changed Winslow Creek to Pine Creek. National Archives photo no. 57-PS-825 (Geological Survey Collection).

54. Jack Hillers on the Aquarius Plateau, July 1875. Photograph probably by Almon Harris Thompson or Grove Karl Gilbert. National Archives photo no. 57-PS-804 (Geological Survey Collection).

then cross, the Escalante Desert, a strip of country lying between the Escalante River on the east and the Kaiparowits Plateau on the west. The party then climbed the Kaiparowits, probably up through an access route in the eastern escarpment now called the Middle Trail by local ranchers. Once on top, Hillers tried to photograph Navajo Mountain, across the chasm of Glen Canyon from the Kaiparowits, but failed due to poor light. The party descended from the plateau, and Hillers photographed the "Goblin" arches (fig. 55) with the Kaiparowits in the background.

Gilbert, Hillers, and others then returned to the Henry Mountains, where Gilbert continued his study of the peaks. In 1877 the Powell Survey published Gilbert's *Geology of the Henry Mountains*. That report, together with Gilbert's subsequent report on Lake Bonneville (the vast Pleistocene lake of which the Great Salt Lake is but a paltry remnant) remain classic studies in American geology. As Gilbert's biographer aptly notes, "The *Henry Mountains* had been a tour de force; *Lake Bonneville* was a summa."[15]

In late September 1875 Thompson and Hillers returned to Washington, D.C. There Hillers began preparing his photographs for the Centennial Exhibition. But Powell and Spencer Baird felt that more photographs were needed, as well as a better representative collection of Hopi artifacts. After pulling some fiscal strings Powell received authorization in early January 1876 to have additional photographs and ethnographic collections made at the Hopi villages in Arizona Territory. Thompson and Hillers were dispatched to do the work. Hillers wrote Powell from St. Louis on January 16 to say that he and Thompson had procured $34 worth of beads and $9 worth of peacock feathers to trade with the Hopi.[16] It is not clear how long the two men were at Hopi, but Hillers obtained some of his best photographs of the Hopi villages during the trip (figs. 77, 78).

The Centennial Exhibition

The Philadelphia extravaganza opened on May 10, 1876, to the grandiose Teutonic strains of the *Centennial Inauguration March,* composed by Richard Wagner for the occasion. According to some reports, the piece mercifully may never have been played again. In the vast Machinery Hall, President Ulysses S. Grant and Dom Pedro, the Emperor of Brazil, pushed a button to start the great Corliss Engine that powered the many machines in the hall. Besides the Machinery Hall, the focal point of the Exhibition, there was much for eager visitors to see. Over ten million visitors, during the next five months and three weeks, saw, among other things, the hand and torch of the Statue of Liberty (put on display to raise money for construction of the base of the statue), the first sewing machine, the first practical typewriter, and Alexander Graham Bell's telephone, although the latter apparently received little attention.[17]

55. The Goblin's Archway,
Escalante Desert, Utah, Sum-
mer 1875. Kaiparowits Plateau
in background. International
Museum of Photography
Collection, Eastman House,
Rochester, New York.

Hillers's photographs were exhibited in the Government Building with the Indian exhibits (where they had to compete with an original copy of the Declaration of Independence, and a great clutter of other exhibits). The Smithsonian exhibit centered on material culture—archaeological and ethnographic specimens from many regions and many Indian tribes. Professional collectors had been commissioned, and they fanned out over the Great Plains, the Southwest, California, the Great Basin, the Northwest Coast, and Alaska. They dug up, or bought up, hundreds of archaeological and ethnographic artifacts and shipped them to Philadelphia for display.[18] The Hayden Survey exhibit included a series of scale models of archaeological sites in the Southwest. In 1874–75, W. H. Jackson and W. H. Holmes of the Hayden Survey had explored the Four Corners region. They had located and recorded a number of spectacular cliff dwellings, although they did not find the great cliff dwellings of the Mesa Verde. (Those would not be seen by whites until the 1880s.) They had also recorded sites in Canyon de Chelly and the Verde Valley in Arizona, including the Montezuma's Castle site (as it is now known). Jackson and W. F. Hoffman made models of several of the sites.[19]

Proposed, but not approved, was a series of "living exhibits"—in effect ethnographic zoos, in which Indians would live in traditional houses, wear traditional costumes, and, presumably, act like traditional Indians for the edification of the multitudinous visitors. But the Congressional money committee balked at the price tag, an estimated $115,000, so papier-mâché and wax mannequins dressed in Indian clothing were substituted. However, private enterprise did provide live Indians. In "Shantyville," an area outside the Exhibition grounds, there was "an Indian encampment with three hundred native Americans from fifty tribes in charge of George Anderson, the famous Texas scout." The Indians were housed next to a "magnificent soda-fountain equipped with seventy-six syrup tubes."[20]

Back in the Government Building, in addition to the mannequins, there were glass cases stuffed with pottery, weapons, and tools of various types, all arranged according to an arbitrary scheme of technological evolution. The exhibit was dominated by a huge sixty-five-foot-long Haida seagoing canoe from the Queen Charlotte Islands, together with some equally spectacular totem poles from several Northwest Coast tribes.

The final set of Indian exhibits centered on photographs. The two featured photographers were William Henry Jackson and John K. Hillers. According to the Exhibition catalog, "the west end of the Government building has been constructed for the insertion of transparencies of photographs on glass and these are of much interest, as being some of the largest views of the kind to be found." The "largest views" were probably Jackson's 20 × 24 inch plates that he made in the Four Corners region in 1875.[21] Hillers's photographs included his portraits of the Cheyenne, Arapaho, and Pawnee "strappen big fellows" from Indian Territory, together with his Hopi photographs and his 1872 and 1873 Southern Paiute pictures. His photographs of members of the Five Civilized Tribes, John Jumper and others, were apparently not used. The Indian exhibits were not well planned and have been viewed by some historians as chaotic and a "failure."[22] But Hillers's and Jackson's photographs were well received and brought wide recognition to both men, establishing them as leading photographers of Indians and the West. Hillers was assigned to the Powell Survey exhibit and spent most of the summer of 1876 at the Exhibition. At its close he returned to Washington to run the Powell Survey photographic laboratory.

During the 1877 and 1878 field seasons Hillers worked primarily in Utah and Arizona. Powell had assigned Gilbert, Thompson, and Clarence Dutton to collect data on how the arid lands of the West could best be utilized. Hillers's job during those two years was primarily logistical—seeing to horses, wagons, and pack mules needed by the geologists in their work. Correspondence between Powell and G. K. Gilbert during the summer and fall of 1878 indicates that Hillers was working with the latter in and around Gunnison and Kanab, Utah.[23]

The data gathered on these trips were used by Powell in his classic *Report on the Arid Region of the United States,* issued in 1878. Powell called for a drastic change in the handling and disposal of the western public domain. He clearly demonstrated that land allocation procedures used farther east were not feasible west of the 100th meridian. The report was the first principal step Powell took in a battle that occupied him for many years: a rational land use plan for the desert West. It was not until after his death that his recommendations were heeded.[24]

Notes

1. The following discussion of the Centennial Exhibition is based on Benedict, *Anthropology of World's Fairs,* Alwood, *Great Exhibitions,* Lockhurst, *Story of Exhibitions,* Maass, *Glorious Enterprise,* McCullough, *World's Fair Midways,* and Rydell, "All the World's a Fair."

2. Wright, *Guide to Indian Tribes,* p. 138.

3. Foreman, *Indian Removal.*

4. Ingalls donated the photographs taken for him by Hillers, together with a catalog of the collection, to the Huntington Library in 1900.

5. Hillers, *Diary,* p. 166.

6. Hillers, *Diary,* p. 158, n. 88.

7. Wright, *Guide to Indian Tribes,* pp. 234–35.

8. Hillers, *Diary,* p. 160.

9. Hillers, *Diary,* pp. 166–67.

10. Hillers, *Diary,* p. 161.

11. Hillers, *Diary,* p. 162.

12. Hillers, *Diary,* pp. 168–71.

13. Woodward, *The Cherokees,* p. 318; Wright, *Guide to Indian Tribes,* p. 62–72.

14. G. K. Gilbert, *Geology of the Henry Mountains.*

15. G. K. Gilbert, *Lake Bonneville;* Pyne, *Grove Karl Gilbert,* p. 44.

16. J. K. Hillers to J. W. Powell, Jan. 16, 1876 (Powell Survey Correspondence).

17. Alwood, *Great Exhibitions,* pp. 54–56.

18. Baird, "International Centennial Exhibition."

19. W. H. Holmes, "Note on the Ancient Remains of Southwestern Colorado," and W. H. Jackson, "Ancient Ruins in Southwestern Colorado" and "Notice of Ruins in Arizona and Utah." See also Ingram, *Centennial Exhibition,* p. 149.

20. McCullough, *World's Fair Midways,* p. 35.

21. Ingram, *Centennial Exhibition,* p. 149; C. S. Jackson, *Picture Maker of the Old West,* pp. 224–25.

22. Trennert, "Grand Failure."

23. G. K. Gilbert to J. W. Powell, July 29, 1878, Oct. 5, 1878, Oct. 18, 1878 (Powell Survey Correspondence); Darrah, *Powell of the Colorado,* pp. 221–36.

24. Darrah, *Powell of the Colorado,* p. 242.

The Survey, The Bureau, and the Southwest, 1879–85

Dual Duty: The Survey and the Bureau

As the year 1879 began Jack Hillers was once again in Washington, D.C., residing at 607 7th St., N.W. He had just turned thirty-five years old and could look back on eighteen years of adventure, danger, and hard work in the Union army and in the West. He had been a professional photographer for seven years. His work was widely known and appreciated. Engravings from his photographs had appeared in *Scribner's Monthly* as well as other magazines of the day, and in government reports. His pictures of Indians of the Southwest, the Canyon Country, and Indian Territory had been seen by hundreds of thousands of visitors to the Government Building at the Centennial Exhibition. Thousands of others had gazed at his work through stereopticon viewers.

In July 1879 Hillers found himself headed west again, this time as part of a team assigned to make extensive studies, artifact collections, and photographs of the Pueblo Indians of New Mexico and Arizona territories. When Hillers started the trip he was still working for Powell, but Powell was working for the Smithsonian Institution, not the Department of the Interior. The four Great Surveys of the 1870s—headed by Powell, King, Hayden, and Wheeler—were gone, superseded by the United States Geological Survey. The new, consolidated Survey was under the direction of Clarence King.

The events leading to these changes were complex and had been developing for five years. The Surveys had competed for public and Congressional support throughout the 1870s. Inevitably there was some duplication of effort and, at times, considerable friction. By 1878 it was clear that a consolidated geological survey was needed and one that would operate on a sound scientific basis.

Powell played an important behind-the-scenes role in the political maneuvering that led Congress to establish the Geological Survey, in a bill passed on March 30, 1879. The bill specified that the Wheeler, Hayden, and Powell Surveys were abolished, effective June 30, 1879. (King's survey had essentially completed its work by that time.) Once the new Survey was created, the battle was on for its directorship. The leading contenders were thought to be Hayden, Powell, and King. Powell supported King, despite public appearances to the contrary. Finally, President Rutherford Hayes appointed King.[1]

Powell, meanwhile, had quietly chosen to pursue his anthropological interests. Ever since his first encounter with Ute Indians in Colorado in 1869, he had become increasingly interested in American Indians and in the nascent discipline of anthropology. Beginning in 1874–75, he had made anthropological research on American Indians a part of the work of his Survey. He used the occasion of the Centennial Exhibition to announce a new publication series, the *Contributions to North American Ethnology*. In 1876 Powell hired two "philologists," or linguists, James Owen Dorsey and Albert Gatschet, and set them to work collecting and collating data toward a comprehensive genetic classification of American Indian languages.

Powell envisioned a federally funded "Ethnologic Bureau," preferably under the administrative shelter of the Smithsonian Institution.[2] Although no confirming correspondence exists, Powell clearly had a tacit understanding with Spencer F. Baird, who had succeeded Joseph Henry as Secretary of the Smithsonian Institution upon the latter's death in 1878. Powell achieved his aim by a masterpiece of legislative indirection. Tucked away in the back of the same Sundry Civil Appropriation Bill that contained clauses creating the Geological Survey was a short item that read:

For completing and preparing for publication the Contributions to North American Ethnology, under the Smithsonian Institution, $20,000: *Provided:* That all of the archives, records and materials relating to the Indians of North America, collected by the Geographical and Geological Survey of the Rocky Mountain Region [i.e., the Powell Survey], shall be turned over to the Smithsonian Institution, that the work may be completed and prepared for publication under its direction; *Provided:* That it shall meet the approval of the Secretary of the Interior and the Secretary of the Smithsonian Institution.[3]

Powell had written the clause and had it inserted in the bill by friends in Congress.

On July 9, 1879, Baird wrote to Powell, asking him "to take charge of the work" of "completing" the *Contributions* series. Powell accepted, had some Bureau of Ethnology letterhead stationery printed, put his faithful chief clerk, James C. Pilling, in charge of the office, and sent Frank Hamilton Cushing, Jack Hillers, and James Stevenson (whose wife, Tilly, went along) to the Southwest. Powell himself then left for the West to serve for six months on a federal lands commission charged with recommending reforms in the management and disposition of the public domain.[4] Cushing's, Stevenson's, and Hillers's assignments were to begin major new anthropological research among the southwestern tribes, to make extensive collections of ethnographic and archaeological artifacts for the Smithsonian, and to create a photographic record of the Indians and the "ruins" of the region. Dorsey and Gatschet, together with Garrick Mallery and Henry C. Yarrow, all of whom became members of Powell's "Corps of Ethnologists," were given other assignments relating to the anthropological study of American Indians. Thus did John Wesley Powell create the Bureau of Ethnology (in 1894 renamed the Bureau of American Ethnology, a political move necessary at the time). In 1880, the Smithsonian received an appropriation "to continue to complete the *Contributions* . . . series." In 1881, the appropriation was for the "normal operations of the Bureau of Ethnology."[5]

Hillers became the Bureau of Ethnology photographer in 1879, at a salary of $1,800 per year. In 1881 he was moved administratively to the Geological Survey at the same salary. But he was still working for Powell, and would henceforth have double duty as both a Bureau and a Survey photographer. The change came about as follows. Clarence King had accepted the directorship of the Geological Survey in 1879. He was a brilliant geologist and well known as perhaps the greatest raconteur of the age, but his heart was not in administration. He thoroughly disliked the trench warfare of Washington politics, as well as the national politics of dealing with the thorny issues of disposal of the public domain, a task assigned to the Survey. In 1881, seeking surcease and *la dolce vita,* King resigned. President James Garfield appointed his old friend John Wesley Powell to be Director of the Geological Survey, with the advice and consent of the U.S. Senate. Powell accepted, with the proviso that he would remain also as Director of the Bureau of Ethnology. Garfield and the Senate concurred.

The move put Powell in charge of two federal research organizations. It also gave him considerable flexibility. He was never able to get the annual appropriation for the Bureau of Ethnology raised substantially. But the Geological Survey had a much bigger budget, and under Powell's careful nurturing that budget increased exponentially in the years after 1881. By taking only one salary for himself, that from the Survey, and by transferring James Stevenson and Jack Hillers to the Survey payroll, Powell freed nearly $11,000 a year for Bureau of Ethnology purposes. From 1881 to 1887 Stevenson was "detailed" to the Bureau for a part of each year to go to the Southwest and collect artifacts for the Smithsonian. Hillers was "detailed" to go with Stevenson, as well as to work as needed with Survey parties in the region. While in Washington, Hillers was "detailed" to the Bureau as needed to photograph delegations of Indians visiting the city. As before, Hillers still worked for Powell. It was simply a matter of to which account Pilling charged Hillers's salary.

Photographing in the Southwest

John Wesley Powell envisioned his nascent Bureau of Ethnology as a means to "organize anthropological research in America."[6] That meant several things, including the conduct of extensive, often long-range ethnographic, linguistic, and archaeological research programs, making large material culture collections throughout the United States and Alaska, and creating a great photographic record of Indians and their lifeways. Powell saw the American Southwest as an ideal place to pursue all these goals.[7]

Powell had been fascinated by the Southwest and its varied Indian populations and cultures since his first visit there in 1870. After making logistical arrangements in southern Utah for the 1871 river trip, Powell had returned east via the Hopi mesas in Arizona and Santa Fe, New Mexico. With Jacob Hamblin he had stopped at Hopi long enough to observe something of the inhabitants' life and ceremonies, which he later described in an article in *Scribner's Monthly,* with illustrations based on Hillers's photographs.[8] Now, in 1879, Powell envisioned a more general study of all the Indian pueblos: Hopi, Zuni, Acoma, and Laguna, and the twenty-some pueblos along the upper Rio Grande from Taos in the north to Isleta, below Albuquerque, in the south (map 3). Ultimately, other non-Pueblo tribes, Navajo, Apache, Havasupai, and others were to be included as well.

Cushing, Stevenson, and Hillers were sent out in 1879 to begin this work. Cushing began what was to become a five-year stay with the Zuni, during which time he became an initiated member of the Bow Priest Society and did remarkable ethnographic work. Stevenson's job was to collect ethnographic artifacts from the various pueblos. Tilly Stevenson became seriously interested in the Indians, particularly the Zuni and the Zia. She began ethnographic work of her own at Zuni, much to Cushing's disgust. He felt she was infringing on his territory. A mutual disregard sprang up between the two that lasted for years.[9] Hillers's task was to make an extensive photographic record of the pueblos and the archaeological ruins of the region. In 1879 he was making his third trip to the Southwest. He had made trips to the Hopi mesas in 1872 and again in 1876, but now his assignment was much broader. In 1879 and the years following, sometimes with Stevenson, sometimes with other Bureau or Survey personnel, he ranged widely over New Mexico and Arizona.

When Hillers and his compatriots arrived in New Mexico in July 1879, they found what would later be termed the Land of Enchantment. It was, and is, a region of stark scenic beauty inhabited by peoples of diverse cultural and historical backgrounds. There were the "Anglos," Euroamericans from the East, including traders, merchants, politicians, Indian agents, U.S. Army officers and soldiers, and ranchers. The traders and merchants first arrived in the 1820s with the opening of the Santa Fe Trail. The army arrived in 1846, bloodlessly acquiring the province of New Mexico from the nation of Mexico. The politicians soon followed, as did the Indian agents, the miners, and more merchants.

There were the Hispanics, descendants of the Spanish and the Mexican Indians who had come to colonize the region after 1598 and later mixed with the indigenous Indian population. There were the various nomadic and seminomadic Indian tribes, principally the Navajo and their linguistic kin, the Apache. For two centuries and more the Navajo and Apache, as well as the Ute, Comanche, Kiowa, and other tribes from the Great Plains, had preyed on the settlements of New Mexico. By 1879 only the Apache were still at large, engaged in a desperate final struggle with the U.S. Army that would not end for another decade.

Finally, there were the Pueblo Indians, peaceful farmers living in a series of villages, or pueblos, strung along the Rio Grande and its tributaries, and at Acoma, Laguna, Zuni, and Hopi to the west (maps 3 and 4). And all around were thousands of ruins, the remains of villages large and small occupied by the various ancestors of the living pueblo dwellers (as we now know) over nearly two millennia.[10]

The pueblos were of particular interest to Stevenson and Hillers because of their rich material culture, complex ceremonies, and photographic potential. During the 1879 field season they collected and photographed at Zuni, Hopi, Laguna, Acoma, Cochiti, Santo Domingo, Tesuque, Santa Clara, San Juan, Jemez, and Old Pecos, and visited some of the spectacular ruins in Canyon de Chelly. In 1880 they confined their efforts to the Rio Grande valley, visiting Taos, San Juan, Santa Clara, San Ildefonso, Nambe, Pojoaque, Cochiti, Jemez, Zia, Santa Ana, Santo Domingo, San Felipe, and Sandia. They apparently did not visit Picuris, high in the Sangre de Cristo Mountains south of Taos. At each pueblo Stevenson purchased pottery, weaving, clothing, ceremonial regalia—whatever he could acquire. Hillers photographed each pueblo and if possible some of its occupants.[11]

In the fall of 1880, the ethnohistorian and archaeologist Adolph F. A. Bandelier began what proved to be a twelve-year career of anthropological and historical research in the Southwest. His path soon crossed that of the Stevensons and Hillers. In his journals Bandelier notes meeting them in September and October 1880, at Santa Fe and at Cochiti Pueblo: "Stevenson, etc. arrived in two buggies [at Cochiti]. . . . Went to the houses of the cacique and governor. Then called on me with his

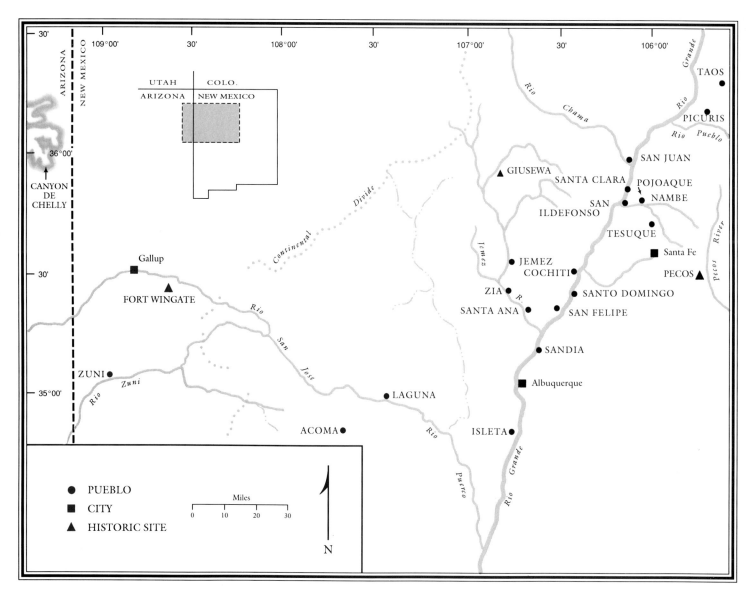

MAP 3. Rio Grande and Adjacent Pueblos.

wife. . . . Hellers [*sic*] . . . [is] with him. They took photographs of the pueblo. Bought many things. . . . They took a photograph of the governor also."[12]

The Rio Grande pueblos have complex prehistories and histories; even today those of some pueblos are not fully understood. Legends and available archaeological and linguistic evidence suggest that the ancestors of the historic Rio Grande pueblos came from the Anasazi area to the northwest and the Mogollon area to the southwest, probably incorporating indigenous groups in the valley after about AD 1100. Linguistically the pueblos belong to two unrelated language families, Keresan and Tanoan. Culturally and socially there are many overall similarities, but each pueblo nonetheless possesses many distinctive features. Most of the present-day villages have been occupied on, or near, their present sites since before the Spanish *Entrada* of 1540.

Spanish settlement of the Rio Grande valley after AD 1598 had enormous and devastating impacts, as the Spanish subjugated the pueblos and tried to replace indigenous religions with Catholicism. The Pueblo Revolt of 1680 drove the Spanish out, but they returned in 1692. Missions were reestablished and the Spanish regained political and economic control. They relinquished that control to Mexico in 1821, and Mexico in turn relinquished it to the United States in 1846. Through it all the pueblos maintained as much of their lifeways and cultural integrity as they could. They still fight to do so.[13]

Hillers's photographs of the Rio Grande pueblos between 1879 and 1882 (e.g., figs. 56–65) are particularly valuable records of how the pueblos appeared at that time. He attempted to systematically photograph each pueblo, although he spent more time, and more glass plates, at some than others.

56. North house cluster, Taos Pueblo, New Mexico, 1880. Taos is the northernmost of the Rio Grande pueblos. The sacred Taos Mountains are seen in the background. Settlement of the site began about AD 1350; there has been continuous occupation since that time. When Coronado visited Taos in 1540, there were multistory structures north and south of the Taos River which bisects the pueblo, as there are today. Because of its proximity to the High Plains, Taos was a center for aboriginal trade between Plains peoples and Puebloans, and Taos culture is a blend of elements from both regions. National Anthropological Archives, Smithsonian Institution (Hillers's album).

57. Santa Clara Pueblo, New
Mexico, 1879 or 1880. The
pueblo has been in its present
location since at least the early
Spanish period. National
Anthropological Archives,
Smithsonian Institution
(Hillers's album).

58. San Ildefonso Pueblo, New
Mexico, 1880. The pueblo may
have been established as early
as AD 1300. The church was
built under the direction of
the Franciscans in 1717. The
kiva, the round, flat-roofed
structure with steps at left
center, is still extant. In this
century, San Ildefonso was the
home of the famed potter, the
late Maria Montoya Martinez.
National Anthropological
Archives, Smithsonian Institution (Hillers's album).

59. Sandia Pueblo, New Mexico, 1880. The rugged Sandia Mountains rise in the background to the east. The area around Sandia was occupied by at least AD 1300, but the present location of the pueblo can only be clearly established back to 1617, when the seat of the mission of San Francisco was established there. Sandia was abandoned during the Pueblo Revolt and was not re-settled until 1748, apparently by a mixed group of refugees from several pueblos. National Anthropological Archives, Smithsonian Institution (Hillers's album).

60. Cochiti Pueblo, New Mexico, 1880. The pueblo has been in the same location in historic times, but little is known about its early history. Cochiti remains one of the most culturally and religiously conservative of the Rio Grande pueblos. National Anthropological Archives, Smithsonian Institution (Hillers's album).

61. Santo Domingo Pueblo, New Mexico, 1880. The pueblo has been occupied since about AD 1300, although it has been rebuilt due to flooding of the Rio Grande. Note the railroad tracks and telegraph poles. Railroads were just being built into the Rio Grande Valley, and on to the west, in the early 1880s. The wagon on the right in the photograph was probably for Hillers's photographic equipment. The other was for the artifacts that James Stevenson was busily collecting. National Anthropological Archives, Smithsonian Institution.

62. San Felipe Pueblo, New
Mexico, 1880. The view is
from the west. The church
was built in 1706. National
Anthropological Archives,
Smithsonian Institution.

63. Pedro Jose Quivera, Governor of San Felipe Pueblo,
New Mexico, demonstrating
a bow drill to perforate beads,
1880. This is one of Hillers's
best-known Southwest photographs. National Anthro-
pological Archives, Smithsonian Institution.

64. Ruins of San Jose Church, Giusewa, New Mexico, 1879. The church of San Jose was founded in 1601 on the site of the Jemez pueblo Giusewa, to the west of the present-day Jemez pueblo. The church was begun by Fray Alonso de Lugo, but was built by Indian slave labor under the supervision of Fray Zarate Salmeron, between 1628 and 1638. The ruins are presently maintained as a New Mexico State Monument. In the photograph, the figures seated on the rock in the center are probably James and Tilly Stevenson; the others are unidentified. The Denver Public Library, Western History Department.

65. Jemez Pueblo, New Mexico, 1879. The Denver Public Library, Western History Department.

Zuni, Hopi, and Canyon de Chelly

In 1881 Hillers and Stevenson concentrated their efforts on the two westernmost pueblos, Zuni and Hopi. Hillers also spent some time with staff members of the Geological Survey that season. At one point, he and the Survey crew ran into Captain John Gregory Bourke near the Mormon settlement of Sunset in northern Arizona. Bourke, famed both as an ethnologist and aide-de-camp to General George Crook, reported that libations were in order. Hillers took charge: "Hillers reappeared with a mixture of ginger and whiskey. The ginger was all right, but the whiskey, from the Mormon town of Brigham, was as vile as Arizona could produce."[14]

Hillers took numerous photographs at Zuni in 1879 and again in 1881, in part to document Frank Hamilton Cushing's extended studies there. The pueblo of Zuni lies on the high plateau area of New Mexico, west of the Continental Divide. In 1879 Zuni consisted of a single, large multistory pueblo with some outlying farmsteads. In 1540 when Francisco Vasquez de Coronado and his men came from Mexico looking for the "Seven Golden Cities of Cibola," they found instead several adobe and rock villages occupied by the Zuni people. Sorely disappointed, the Spanish looked elsewhere for golden cities, or even just gold; finding none they returned to Mexico. Other Spanish returned in 1598, to settle and to dominate the Zuni and other pueblos. The domination, the Pueblo Revolt, its aftermath, and other factors had, by the nineteenth century, reduced the Zuni people to a single village, Zuni.[15]

Hillers's photographs of Zuni provide exceptional coverage of the pueblo and its people in a narrow space of time. Those used here (figs. 66–75) represent only a small fraction of his photographs at the pueblo.

66. View over rooftops, Zuni Pueblo, New Mexico, 1879. National Anthropological Archives, Smithsonian Institution.

67. Drying crops on rooftops,
Zuni Pueblo, New Mexico,
1879. National Anthropological Archives, Smithsonian
Institution.

68. *Wall Coping and Oven*,
Zuni Pueblo, New Mexico,
1879. National Anthropological Archives, Smithsonian
Institution.

69. Zuni Pueblo, New Mexico,
1879. National Anthropological Archives, Smithsonian
Institution (Hillers's album).

70. *Method of Transportation
and Pack Animals*, Zuni
Pueblo, New Mexico, 1879.
National Anthropological
Archives, Smithsonian
Institution.

71. *The Dance,* Zuni Pueblo,
New Mexico, 1879. The struc-
ture on the right is the re-
mains of a Catholic church
built after the 1680 revolt.
National Anthropological
Archives, Smithsonian
Institution.

72. Koyemshi, or Mudheads,
in plaza, Zuni Pueblo, New
Mexico, 1879. During ceremonial dances Koyemshi accompany kachina dancers to the
plaza, provide cues for the
dancers, and act as clowns
between dances. National
Anthropological Archives,
Smithsonian Institution
(Hillers's album).

73. Pedro Pino, former Governor of Zuni Pueblo, New Mexico, 1879. Pino had been Governor of Zuni in the 1840s and 1850s and had welcomed contingents of the U.S. Army that called at the pueblo during those years. National Anthropological Archives, Smithsonian Institution.

74. Governors of Zuni Pueblo, New Mexico, 1879. This is a group portrait of the council of secular leaders who dealt with political and external affairs, as contrasted with the priests, who dealt with religious matters and were usually unknown to outsiders. Prior to Spanish times, the priests ruled in all things, but the necessity of protecting the indigenous religion from Spanish persecution led to the creation of secular "governors," or front men, who were ostensible leaders and dealt with the outside world. National Anthropological Archives, Smithsonian Institution.

75. Children with teachers at Zuni Pueblo, 1879. The man on the right is Taylor F. Ealey, a Presbyterian missionary-schoolteacher who, with his wife Mary, spent two frustrating years at Zuni in 1879-81. (See Bender, *Missionaries, Outlaws and Indians,* pp. 79-167.) He often clashed with Frank Hamilton Cushing, who opposed Ealey's attempts to "civilize" the Zuni. The woman on the left is Jennie Hammaker, Ealey's assistant teacher. Four of the children in the photograph, two boys and two girls, were later sent to Carlisle Indian School in Pennsylvania. They were given names Taylor Ealey, Mary Ealey, Jennie Hammaker, and Frank Cushing. (See Bender, p. 74, and Fleming and Luskey, *North American Indians in Early Photographs,* pp. 74, 92-93.) The tall person in the center is Wewhe (see also fig. 101), a male transvestite. As in other Indian societies, Zuni men could adopt women's roles in certain circumstances. National Anthropological Archives, Smithsonian Institution (Hillers's album).

From Zuni, Hillers and Stevenson journeyed westward to the Hopi mesas (map 4) in the fall of 1881—Hillers's fourth visit there in less than a decade. In 1872, during his first visit with Clem Powell and Jacob Hamblin, Hillers had recorded his impressions in his diary, including a meal with a Hopi family at Oraibi on Third Mesa:

In the evening Jacob and I were invited to sup. We accepted. After climbing up a ladder to the second story we were shown a place on a sheep skin. A huge earthen pot set on two stones over a small fire boiling. Directly on, a huge bowl was set in front of us. It was filled up from the pot on the fire, which proved to be corn and mutton boiled into a soup. A waiter tray made of willows was next placed on the ground. An armful of cornbread resembling paper cinders rolled up [*piki* bread] was next placed on the ground. Three mellons were brought from a large stack in the corner. Everything was now ready. Three men and three women seated themselves likewise on a sheepskin. The old man gave the signal for commencement, by diving his hand into the bowl of soup—hunted out the biggest piece of mutton. The rest followed suit. Being very hungry myself, and as the old saying is, When you are in Rome you must do as the Romans do, so I sailed in with my digits and pulled forth a dumplin. Jacob told me not to eat, as it was prepared by the virgin of the house, who had chewed every bit before it was put into the pot. I asked what for. He told me, to arouse the animal passion of the young warrior and so hasten her marriage. I allowed the dumplin to roll back, and fetched forth a leg, or rather part of a leg of mutton. I done justice to the meal. I watched the dumplin but none appeared to want it so it was left in the pot. The maiden gave a sigh.[16]

Hillers kept his bachelor status, as he had earlier with the young widow in Georgia, and would again (barely) with the charming Alvoretta Jerome in Indian Territory in 1875. His description of Oraibi, as it appeared in 1872, is worth repeating in relation to his photographs:

They build their houses on top of the cliff here in Oriby. There are three streets running parallel to each other. Houses are built of stone and clay for mortar—all joining each other, generally two stories high. A ladder is placed on the ground to the top of the first. The second story is set back, allowing a space of eight feet or more to walk on. From this you go into the second story, which has a door. A hole is made in the top of the first and a ladder placed in the hole to get down by. In summer they live in the upper story and in winter in the lower. They cultivate the land, raise corn, beans, mellons, peppers and peaches. Raise lots of sheep, asses, a few horses and cattle. Men wear their hair long

behind and even cut with the eyes in front. While at work they are naked excepting a breach clout. The women wear their hair long and done up in a long role hanging down each side. Wear a black blanket dress fastened over one shoulder and a sash—that is the married ones. The marriageable wear their clothes the same. Their hair is done up on the side in the shape of a ram's horn, and are as a general thing pretty—fine features.[17]

When Hillers visited the Hopis he encountered a people whose ancestors had been in the general area for millennia. But the historic Hopi pueblos he visited, perched high on the three mesas, "on top of the cliff," were where they were as a result of a long and complex history. The thirteenth century was a time of drought and arroyo cutting in much of the Southwest. Seeking still-arable lands, people migrated from the Marsh Pass and Black Mesa areas to the north, and from the Flagstaff and Little Colorado areas to the west and south, to the foot of the three mesas now occupied. Springs along the escarpment made it possible to farm. It was also possible to raise crops on Antelope Mesa to the east. With the advent of the Spanish, in 1629 a mission was established at Awatovi, along Tallahogan Wash on Antelope Mesa. After the 1680 Pueblo Revolt, the Hopis moved from the escarpment terraces and Antelope Mesa onto the three high mesa tops for defense. The Spanish were never able to regain control of the Hopi villages; the Hopis fended them off in 1701 and 1716. During the Pueblo Revolt, the Hopis took in a group of refugees from the Rio Grande region who established the village of Hano on the easternmost mesa.[18]

The Hopi mesas, from east to west, are called by anthropologists First, Second, and Third mesas. In 1872 there were three villages on the narrow top of First Mesa, the Tewa (Rio Grande refugee) village of Hano and the Hopi villages of Sichomovi and Walpi (fig. 76). Mishongnovi, Shipaulovi, and Shongopavi (fig. 79) were the villages on Second Mesa, and Oraibi (fig. 80) was the principal village on Third Mesa (map 4).

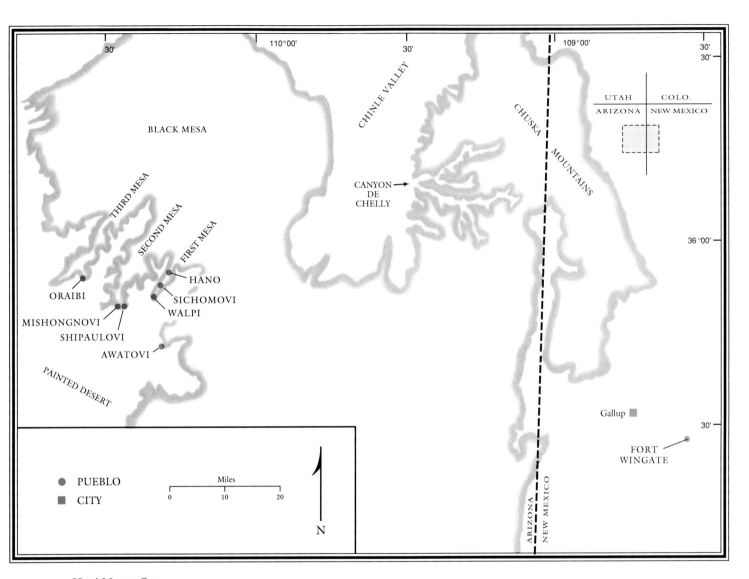

MAP 4. Hopi Mesas, Canyon de Chelly, and Adjacent Regions, Arizona-New Mexico.

76. Hopi mesas. View southward on First Mesa from
Hano, with Sichomovi in the
middle distance and Walpi at
the end of the mesa, 1879 or
1881. National Anthropological Archives, Smithsonian
Institution.

77. Hopi pueblo of Walpi, First Mesa, Arizona. Note sheep pens along the side of the escarpment. This photograph in a slightly different format was exhibited at the Philadelphia Centennial Exhibition, 1876. National Anthropological Archives, Smithsonian Institution.

78. Dance Rock at Walpi
Pueblo, Arizona. This is a
well-known Hillers photo-
graph. It was exhibited at
the Philadelphia Centennial
Exhibition, 1876. National
Anthropological Archives,
Smithsonian Institution.

79. Hopi pueblos of Mish-
ongnovi (foreground) and
Shipaulovi, Arizona, 1879 or
1881. Figure in center is probably James Stevenson. National
Anthropological Archives,
Smithsonian Institution.

80. Hopi house and occupants, Oraibi, Third Mesa, Arizona, 1879. National Anthropological Archives, Smithsonian Institution.

81. Hopi man weaving, Walpi, Arizona, 1879. This is a well-known Hillers photograph. National Anthropological Archives, Smithsonian Institution.

82. Hopi man using spindle-whorl, Walpi, Arizona, 1879. National Anthropological Archives, Smithsonian Institution.

83. Three Hopi women fixing their hair, Walpi, Arizona, 1879. National Anthropological Archives, Smithsonian Institution.

84. Two unmarried Hopi women, Walpi, Arizona, 1879. The women's whorled "butterfly" (or "ram's horns," as Hillers called them) hairdos and cornmeal-covered faces signify their unmarried status. National Anthropological Archives, Smithsonian Institution.

85. *Modisi,* Hopi woman, Walpi, Arizona, 1879. National Anthropological Archives, Smithsonian Institution.

86. *Sallie,* Hopi woman, Walpi, Arizona, 1879. The hairdo indicates the woman is married. National Anthropological Archives, Smithsonian Institution.

87. *Big Navajo,* Navajo (?) or
Hopi woman, Walpi, Arizona,
1879. National Anthropological Archives, Smithsonian
Institution.

88. Canyon de Chelly, Arizona, 1879 or 1881. National Archives photo no. 57-PS-87 (Geological Survey Collection).

89. *Captains of the Canyon* (Spider Rock), Canyon de Chelly, Arizona, 1879 or 1881. National Archives photo no. 57-PS-88 (Geological Survey Collection).

90. Canyon de Chelly, Arizona, 1879 or 1881. National Archives photo no. 57-PS-92 (Geological Survey Collection).

91. White House Ruin, Canyon de Chelly, Arizona, 1881. The Denver Public Library, Western History Department.

From the Hopi mesas, Hillers and Stevenson traveled northeast to Canyon de Chelly in the heart of Navajo country. In prehistoric times the Anasazi (ancestors of the Hopi, and possibly other Pueblo groups) lived in the canyon. Remains of their villages, including Mummy Cave (figs. 92, 93) and White House Ruin (fig. 91) are found throughout the canyon and its tributaries. Later, after about AD 1500, the Navajo came to the canyon, at first to farm, and after the Spanish arrival to herd sheep as well. In the 1860s the Navajos hid in the canyon from Colonel Kit Carson and his troops. But they were tracked down, many were killed, and some 3,000 survivors were marched off to four years' imprisonment at Fort Sumner in the Bosque Redondo in the Pecos Valley, New Mexico.

Canyon de Chelly has inspired Anglo visitors since a detachment of U.S. Army soldiers explored it in 1849. Both W. H. Jackson and Timothy O'Sullivan photographed there in the early 1870s. Hillers followed them in 1879, 1881, and 1882. Professional and amateur photographers alike have since gazed in awe at the canyon and tried to capture its eerie fascination on film. Like portions of Glen Canyon, now drowned beneath Lake Powell, the red-rust and magenta Navajo Sandstone cliffs and spires of de Chelly produce a sense of wonder. Hillers's photographs convey that wonder as eloquently as any done since.

Hillers spent the 1882 field season with Stevenson, partly in Canyon de Chelly and partly around Fort Win-

CAVE AR

92. Canyon del Muerto from
Mummy Cave, Arizona, 1881.
The Denver Public Library,
Western History Department.

93. Mummy Cave ruins, Canyon del Muerto, Arizona,
1881. International Museum
of Photography, Eastman
House, Rochester, New York.

94. Fort Wingate, New Mexico, 1882. The fort was established in 1860 at the north end of the Zuni Mountains, east of Zuni Pueblo, as part of the U.S. army's campaign to quell the Navajo. It was initially named Fort Fauntleroy, for a colonel by that name who subsequently joined the Confederate army, to the embarrassment of those who had named the fort for him. It was renamed Fort Wingate after the Civil War, for Captain Benjamin Wingate, who died in the war—on the Union side. National Archives photo no. 57-PS-113 (Geological Survey Collection).

gate in western New Mexico. In both areas they concentrated on archaeological sites, but Hillers also recorded Fort Wingate itself (figs. 94–96).

In 1883 Hillers accompanied A. H. Thompson to the Southwest, where the latter did some mapping and geological work. In early September 1883, Powell wrote to Thompson that "Hillers may take pictures where he pleases until further orders."[19] A shot of the recently completed railroad trestle over Canyon Diablo, in Arizona (fig. 97), may be an example of doing as he pleased.[20]

Ending His Bachelor's Resolve

Hillers left Arizona in mid-September 1883 and traveled to New York, where he finally gave up his "bachelor's resolve" and was married, at age forty. On September 28, 1883, in the famed St. Matthews Lutheran Church in Manhattan, "Johann Heinrich [sic] Hillers, single, of Brinkum, Hannover, and widow [?] Elizabeth Schierenbeck, of Leste, Hannover on the 28th of September, 1883

through the undersigned in the presence of witnesses Philipp Wilhelm Judd and Nette Kohlweih have been joined in matrimony [as is] hereby officially confirmed at St. Matthews Church, New York C. 29 Sept. A.D. 1883." Officiating was the Reverend J. H. Sicker.[21]

Elizabeth Kneif Schierenbeck was the widow of Henry Schierenbeck, who had died in New York City in 1879. Very little is known about her. It is not clear whether Hillers knew her when they were children in Hanover or from his early days in New York. Since they were both from Hanover, their families may have settled close to each other in New York. It is equally unclear whether Hillers had kept in touch with Elizabeth during his years in the army and the West, and hers as a married woman in New York. Presumably they did keep in touch, decided to wed after she was widowed, and did so. The couple returned to Washington, D.C., and within a year or so settled down at 238 First St., S.E., on Capitol Hill. In January 1888 they had a son, John Kenna Hillers, their only child.

95. *Navajo Church,* near Fort Wingate, New Mexico, 1882. National Archives photo no. 57-PS-96 (Geological Survey Collection).

NAVAJO CHURCH, NEAR FORT

96. Ruins near Fort Wingate, New Mexico, 1882. The remains of a prehistoric structure, probably for food storage. The Denver Public Library, Western History Department.

97. Railroad trestle over Canyon Diablo, Arizona, 1883. National Archives photo no. 57-PS-109 (Geological Survey Collection).

98. San Francisco Mountains,
Arizona, 1885. National Ar-
chives photo no. 57-PS-104
(Geological Survey
Collection).

The Last Southwest Trip

Hillers did not go to the field in 1884, presumably taking some time to get settled in Washington. But in 1885 he again found himself in the Southwest, on a trip with Powell. It would be the last trip for both to the region. Although the trip was an official one for scientific purposes, it was probably something of a vacation for Powell, who by 1885 was deep in wrenching political battles over the use and disposal of the public domain. It was likely also a journey of nostalgia for both men. By 1885 it was possible to travel all the way to Flagstaff, Arizona, by train—far different from Powell's and Hillers's trips by horseback or wagon a decade earlier. Near Flagstaff, Hillers photographed the San Francisco Mountains (fig. 98), which rise majestically above the town. Perhaps both Powell and Hillers recalled that, according to the Hopi, the sacred Kachina spirits live on the tops of the San Francisco peaks, journeying northeastward yearly to the Hopi mesas to participate in the ceremonies in their honor. In Walnut Canyon, near Flagstaff, the two visited some of the small cliff dwellings in the canyon walls (fig. 99). The canyon is now within Walnut Canyon National Monument.

The two men also paid a visit to the South Rim of the Grand Canyon, just beginning to be developed as a tourist attraction. One wonders what their thoughts and words were as they gazed down into the great chasm they had so perilously explored. Somewhere down there, Hillers had saved Powell's life in a boiling rapid, even more firmly cementing the close bond between the two. Down there too Hillers had aggravated his old back injury from Civil War days. It had plagued him ever since, as he jounced through Indian Territory, the Canyon Country, and the Southwest on horseback and in wagons. In a few years it would become a severe problem, and would remain so for the rest of his life. At the end of the trip, the two returned to Washington, D.C. Neither would see the Southwest again—except in their mind's eye, and in Hillers's photographs.

99. Cliff dwellings, Walnut Canyon, Arizona, 1885. National Archives photo no. 57-PS-102 (Geological Survey Collection).

Notes

1. The complex creation of the Geological Survey and the roles Powell played during its inception are discussed in detail in Darrah, *Powell of the Colorado*, pp. 237–54, Stegner, *Beyond the Hundredth Meridian*, pp. 203–51, and Wilkins, *Clarence King*, pp. 230–65.

2. Fowler and Fowler, "John Wesley Powell, Anthropologist," p. 164.

3. *United States Statutes*, XX, 397.

4. Powell had fired his first salvo on the public lands issue in his 1878 *Report on the Lands of the Arid Region*. He would continue to be actively embroiled in the issues relating to the rational use of public lands for the next fifteen years.

5. For Powell's founding of the Bureau of Ethnology see Fowler and Fowler, "John Wesley Powell, Anthropologist," pp. 164–68, Hinsley, *Savages and Scientists*, pp. 145–89, Judd, *Bureau of American Ethnology*, and Flack, *Desideratum in Washington*, pp. 107–42.

6. J. W. Powell, "Report of the Director," *First Annual Report*, p. xii.

7. For histories of anthropological research in the Southwest see Schroeder, "History of Archaeological Research," Basso, "History of Ethnological Research," and Gaede, *Camera, Spade and Pen*.

8. J. W. Powell, "Ancient Province of Tusayan."

9. For Cushing's work at Zuni and his relations with Tilly Stevenson, see Brandes, "Frank Hamilton Cushing," Hinsley, "Ethnographic Charisma and Scientific Routine," and Mark, "Frank Hamilton Cushing." After James Stevenson's death in 1887, Powell hired Tilly (who changed her name for publications purposes to Matilda Coxe Stevenson) as a member of the Bureau staff. She ultimately produced major monographs on her researches at Zuni and Zia pueblos: M. C. Stevenson, "The Sia" and "The Zuni Indians."

10. For overviews of southwestern anthropology see Sturtevant, *Handbook of North American Indians*, vols. 9–10.

11. J. Stevenson, "Illustrated Catalogue."

12. Bandelier, *Southwestern Journals*, p. 178.

13. For detailed discussions of the several Rio Grande pueblos see articles on them in Sturtevant, *Handbook of North American Indians* 9:255–429.

14. Bourke, *Snake Dance*, p. 354.

15. Woodbury, "Zuni Prehistory and History to 1850"; Crampton, *The Zunis of Cibola*.

16. Hillers, *Diary*, p. 150.

17. Hillers, *Diary*, p. 151.

18. For overviews of Hopi history and culture see Brew, "Hopi Prehistory and History to 1850," and Frigout, "Hopi Ceremonial Organization."

19. J. W. Powell to A. H. Thompson, Sept. 1, 1883 (Powell Survey Correspondence).

20. Compare Hillers's photograph of the Canyon Diablo trestle with that taken, possibly in the same year, by Ben Wittick (Packhard and Packhard, *Southwest 1880 with Ben Wittick*, p. 35) and with a stereograph taken by an unknown photographer in 1903 (Earle, *Points of View*, p. 47, top).

21. One of the documents in Hillers Records gives his date of marriage as "Sept. 28, 1884." However, the marriage certificate is clearly dated "Sept. 28, 1883" (photocopy in the author's possession). At the time of writing, the records of St. Matthews Church in New York City, where other Hillers family records may be, were not available.

Jack Hillers in Washington, 1885–1900

Laboratory Work and Indian Portraits

Back in Washington after the 1885 trip, Hillers resumed two tasks he had carried out since 1879. One was supervising the photographic laboratory for both the Geological Survey and the Bureau of Ethnology. The second was photographing Indian leaders visiting the city.

By 1885, other photographers were employed by the Survey and occasionally by the Bureau. The advent of successful dry-plate photography after 1880–81 made photography, while still a complex process, much less cumbersome than the wet-plate process that Hillers, Jackson, O'Sullivan, and others had used. The principal benefit was that the photographer did not have to carry a dark tent, or a specially equipped darkroom wagon, along in the field. Plates could be exposed and returned to a central laboratory for processing and printing. The change also meant many more photographs were taken by Geological Survey field parties, which in turn meant much more darkroom work for Hillers and his assistants, as indicated in an *Annual Report:*

Photography is used by the Survey for a variety of purposes. Many negatives are taken by working geologists in the field for purposes of illustrating geological phenomena. A photographic laboratory has been organized, under the charge of Mr. J. K. Hillers in which photography is used as an aid in changing the scale of charts and preparing various illustrations for the reports. During the year [1883–84], 536 negatives, 6,231 prints, and 94 transparencies have been made in the laboratory. . . . Mr. Hillers has undertaken no field work during the year, but complete dry-plate outfits have been furnished to a number of field parties, and thus hundreds of valuable negatives from all parts of the country have been added to the collection.[1]

Hillers's second task was to make photographic portraits of prominent Indians visiting Washington. Among the many curious actions taken by the U.S. government throughout the nineteenth century to cope with the "Indian Problem" was to transport Indian leaders to Washington to meet the current Great Father, the incumbent President.[2] Actually, the United States was following British precedent. During the eighteenth century, prominent Indians had been taken to London at various times. The U.S. practice began during Washington's presidency and escalated throughout the nineteenth century. (Prominent Indian leaders still go to Washington on tribal business, although they are no longer shepherded by Indian agents; and they rarely meet with the Great Father.) The theory of both the British and the nineteenth-century U.S. officials was that the Indians would be so impressed with the white man's civilization that they would return home and convince their fellows to lay down their arms, accept whatever reservation lands and other pittances the government might give them, and become "good Christian farmers in overalls." The sordid history of U.S.-Indian relations throughout the nineteenth century, and well beyond, certainly disproved the theory. Nevertheless the practice ritually continued, and in fact increased, throughout the century, as the frontier moved ever westward and more Indian tribes were encountered.

Members of the Indian delegations to Washington endured, and sometimes enjoyed, meeting the current Great Father, touring factories, arsenals, and shipyards, attending plays and concerts, donning white man's clothing—and having their portraits done. Early nineteenth-century Indian visitors sat for their portraits, painted by Charles B. F. J. de St.-Memin, Charles Bird

King, and other prominent artists of the day. Once photographic portraiture was established, Indian delegates were depicted by means of the new medium.[3]

Indians visiting Washington apparently began to be photographed in 1857. One of the first was the Cherokee leader John Ross, uncle of William Potter Ross whom Hillers photographed in Indian Territory in 1875. John Ross first visited Washington in 1831 to plead for his people's rights before the U.S. Supreme Court. Instead of rights, the Cherokees and other southeastern Indians got the federal Indian Removal policy and were forcibly sent to Indian Territory. John Ross died in Washington in 1866, still pleading for his people's rights.[4]

After an initial start at photographing Indians at the McClees Studio in 1857–58, the practice apparently went into abeyance for a decade.[5] When it was resumed in the 1860s, prominent Washington photographers who made Indian portraits included Alexander Gardner, Zeno Shindler, and C. M. Bell. When John Wesley Powell established the Bureau of Ethnology in 1879, the task of photographing visiting Indians fell largely to the Bureau, and particularly to Hillers when he was not in the field.

Between 1879 and 1894 Hillers took dozens of portraits of visiting Indian leaders. Together with many other photographs made by other government as well as private photographers of nineteenth-century Washington, they form a body of work that is of great historic importance. In 1884, probably at Powell's prompting, Secretary of the Interior H. M. Teller issued the following order: "Agents, interpreters and others in charge of Indian delegations visiting Washington will, while not officially engaged on business in this Department, report with the Indians under their charge to the Bureau of Ethnology for purposes of furnishing ethnologic, linguistic and historical information in relation to the tribes in which said Indians belong, and to afford that Bureau an opportunity for obtaining photographs of the visiting Indians."[6] In 1887 Powell reported that whenever possible the Bureau took advantage of the visits of Indian delegations to photograph them: "These are generally the prominent men of the tribes represented by them, and their photographs have biographic and historic interest as well as anthropologic importance. Mr. J. K. Hillers has been in charge of this branch of the work, and during the last year has secured 99 photographs of prominent Indians in both full face and profile, in order to exhibit to better advantage all their facial characteristics. The subjects were from the fol-lowing tribes, viz: White Mountain Apache, 15 persons; Chiricahua Apache, 20; Jicarilla Apache, 8; Sac and Fox, 7; Ute, 4; Shawnee, 9; Omaha, 20; Dakota, 11; Oto and Missouri, 5."[7]

As an indication of some government officials' views of their charges, in 1892 J. G. Morgan, Commissioner of Indian Affairs, wrote to Powell: "A Yakima Indian has just reported to this Office, dressed in barbaric splendor. He is staying at Beveridge's. I think you may be glad to photograph him."[8]

Of the hundreds of Indian portraits Hillers made over the years, only a few representative examples can be included here (figs. 100–105).[9]

Hillers's Last Field Trips

In between Indian delegations, Hillers continued to supervise the Geological Survey photographic laboratory. The workload increased each year, and his health began to deteriorate seriously. In 1891 he filed his first forms with the Pension Bureau, seeking compensation and medical help for what would now be called a service-related disability—his chronic back problem.[10] Nonetheless, he was still well enough to make two more major field trips. The first of these was to the Yosemite Valley and Kings River areas of California in 1892.

The purpose of the California trip cannot clearly be ascertained from the Geological Survey files (again, the paper trail is thin). It is likely that Powell planned to use the photographs in the Geological Survey display at the Chicago World's Columbian Exposition the following year. Whatever the reason, Hillers returned with a number of exquisite photographs of Yosemite Valley, Kings Canyon, and the Big Trees in Mariposa Grove. Of those shown here, Hillers chose the views in figs. 108–110 for his personal album.

The first white man who glimpsed the breathtaking splendor of Yosemite valley, from the canyon rim, was Joseph Reddeford Walker during his traverse of the Great Basin and the Sierra Nevada in 1833.[11] In 1851, a group of whites led by Major James D. Savage stumbled onto the valley while pursuing a group of "U-za-ma-ti" Indians. Soon, "Yosemite" (a Miwok Indian word meaning "grizzly bear" or "killer") was visited by tourists, the first in 1855.[12] By 1859 C. L. Weed was photographing the valley, soon to be followed by Carleton E. Watkins. They in

100. Chato, Chiricahua
Apache, Washington, D.C.,
1886. Chato was a major figure
in the Chiricahua Apache battles against the whites, Mexicans, and the U.S. Army, on
both sides of the U.S.-Mexico
border, between 1866 and
1886. He surrendered to General George Crook in early
February 1884, soon after the
surrender of Geronimo. He
became a sergeant in the
Army scouts, attempting to
bring the rest of his people to
peace. In 1886 he and a party
visited Washington, where he
was given a Peace Medal and
Hillers made his portrait. On
his return to Arizona, he was
rewarded for his services by
being arrested and shipped off
to Florida with Geronimo and
most of the Chiricahua. He
died in 1934 in Arizona, in an
automobile accident. National
Anthropological Archives,
Smithsonian Institution.

101. Wewhe, Zuni male transvestite, Washington, D.C., 1884-87. He was one of Matilda Coxe (Tilly) Stevenson's informants. He was brought to Washington sometime between 1884 and 1887 to assist in setting up some displays for the U.S. National Museum. (See M.C. Stevenson, "The Zuni Indians," and Basso, "History of Ethnological Research," p. 19, fig. 18.) National Anthropological Archives, Smithsonian Institution.

102. Pianaronit, or Big Looking Glass, Comanche, Washington, D.C., 1894. National Anthropological Archives, Smithsonian Institution.

103. Munche Khanche, Missouri, Washington, D.C., 1890-91. Munche Khanche was also known as Big Black Bear and Joseph Powell. He is wearing an early Peace Medal, dated ca. 1798, but one that was probably never awarded. "Extra" Peace Medals were sold by various merchants until after 1900. National Anthropological Archives, Smithsonian Institution.

104. Soquee-Omuce, or Brocky, Piegan, Washington, D.C., 1891-92. He was also known as Heavy Runner. He was one of 252 Piegans who signed a treaty in February 1887 at the Blackfeet Agency in Montana, which redefined Blackfeet territory. He and four other men were taken to Washington in December 1891 as a "reward" for their efforts to achieve self-sufficiency for their people. The trip was apparently made at the suggestion of George Bird Grinnell, the famed Plains Indian ethnographer and ethnohistorian. The photograph was probably taken in the Bureau of Ethnology offices in late December 1891 or early January 1892. National Anthropological Archives, Smithsonian Institution.

105. Tah-ha-chet, or John Hill, Salish or Flathead, Washington, D.C., 1894. He was also known as Shot in the Hand, and Hand Shot Off. He was part of a Flathead delegation to Washington in early 1894. National Anthropological Archives, Smithsonian Institution.

106. View down Yosemite Valley, California, El Capitan on right, 1892. National Archives photo no. 57-PS-35 (Geological Survey Collection).

107. Yosemite Valley, California, 1892. National Archives photo no. 200S-JH-10 (Geological Survey Collection, Hillers's album).

108. *Yosemite Falls during Dry Season*, 1892. National Archives photo no. 57-PS-41 (Geological Survey Collection, Hillers's album).

109. *Yosemite, Home of the Storm Gods,* 1892. National Archives photo no. 57-PS-37 (Geological Survey Collection).

110. Big Trees in Mariposa Grove, California, 1892. National Archives photo no. 57-PS-43 (Geological Survey Collection).

turn were followed by a host of other photographers over the years.[13]

When Hillers arrived in Yosemite in 1892, his practiced eye chose many of the same spots from which to make photographs as had his predecessors. For example, Hillers's photograph of El Capitan (fig. 106) may be compared with photographs taken twenty-eight years earlier from nearly the same location by Weed and Watkins.[14] Hillers's other photographs of Yosemite (figs. 107–109), as well as of the Big Trees (fig. 110), also had many precursors.

In 1893 Hillers spent his time in the Survey photographic laboratory, processing and printing the ever-increasing number of photographs he was given and preparing transparencies for various exhibits, including that at Chicago. In the fall of 1894 he made his last field trip: "In connection with the preparation of the Department of the Interior exhibit at the Cotton States and International Exposition at Atlanta, Mr. Hillers spent two months in the States of North Carolina, Tennessee, Georgia and Florida, taking photographic views. More than one hundred fine negatives of subjects illustrating the mineral resources and industries of the southern states were obtained."[15] Again, there is very little documentation of the trip, only the above note. Captions on the photographs indicate Hillers visited West Virginia and Kentucky, in addition to the states listed.

As indicated, part of Hillers's assignment was to take photographs illustrating the mineral industries of the Southeast; hence the pictures of the ore pit and the blast furnace (figs. 114, 115). But he also took many scenery shots, for example Hickory Nut Gap (fig. 112), one of the principal routes through the Blue Ridge Mountains in western North Carolina. The Gap is noted for its splendid scenery, its "massive upright cliffs, immense boulders, dizzy heights, roaring cascades, lofty waterfalls, peculiar caverns, mountains of rock and curious formations."[16] In 1540 the Spanish expedition led by Hernando de Soto passed through the Gap en route to the Mississippi River. In 1566 another Spanish party, a detachment from the Spanish fort of San Felipe, near Port Royal, also explored the Gap. In 1670, John Lederer probably passed through during his famous exploration of Carolina. In 1673 an expedition led by James Needham and Gabriel Arthur traversed it on its way to the Cherokee towns in present-day Tennessee.[17] Hillers thus included the Gap both for its scenic grandeur and its historic importance.

Finally, one of his southeastern photographs (fig. 117) reflects Hillers's interest in rivers, streams, and waterfalls. The view is of Tallulah Falls on the Tallulah River, which runs through Rabun and Habersam counties in northern Georgia.[18]

Final Years

Following the Southeast trip, Hillers confined his activities to the Survey laboratory, his marriage, and his growing son, John K., Jr. He was increasingly plagued by his back problem and a general deterioration of health. The scope of the laboratory work is indicated in the Survey *Annual Reports*. During 1896–97 the laboratory developed 3,176 negatives, ranging in size from 4 × 5 inches to 28 × 34 inches, and made 13,280 prints, "in the same range." In 1898–99, some 5,856 negatives "in the same range" were developed, together with 18,278 prints.[19]

Perhaps due to the increasing workload, the Survey laboratory began to suffer what would now be called problems of quality control. On November 23, 1899, the laboratory was placed under a committee, "for the purpose of ascertaining the possibilities of improving the quality of the work." On January 1, 1900, the laboratory was placed in charge of one S. J. Kubell, "chief of the Division of Engineering and Printing." In April 1900 Hillers was "transferred to the per diem roll," that is, to part-time, and a new permanent laboratory head appointed.[20]

It is not clear from the Survey files what the problems were in the laboratory. It likely was a combination of factors, only one of which was quality control. Powell had been forced to resign as Director of the Geological Survey in 1894 (he stayed on as Director of the Bureau of American Ethnology until his death in 1902). Thus, Hillers's great friend was no longer head of the Survey, and his overall power in Washington was waning, although his prestige remained high. Part of Hillers's being eased out may have been the common Washington phenomenon of the new guard pushing out the old guard. Hillers's health, however, was probably the dominant factor. His Pension Bureau records reflect deteriorating health and the continuation of the back problem. Then too, by 1900 Hillers was fifty-seven years old, relatively old in the demographics of the turn-of-the-century United States. He had led a strenuous life for nearly four decades, in the army and in the West.

Time and strain caught up with Hillers, as they did with Powell. The latter suffered his first stroke in 1900. Legend at the Smithsonian is that the immediate cause of Powell's stroke was one of many violent arguments he had with the indomitable Matilda Coxe Stevenson, whose will equaled his own. In September 1902 Powell was felled by a second stroke. Hillers was one of the honorary pall bearers at the funeral. A unique comradeship, begun through a chance meeting thirty-one years earlier in Salt Lake City, was ended.

Hillers remained on the per diem roll of the Survey laboratory until 1919, although his Pension Bureau records indicate that after about 1913–15 his health was very poor. Elizabeth Hillers died in October 1913. John K. Hillers, Jr., himself a government photographer for the Bureau of Roads throughout his career, married, and after about 1918 he and his wife, Lila, moved to the house on First Street to care for Jack.

By about 1920 Hillers had become essentially helpless and senile. The family hired a male attendant to help care for him. On November 14, 1925, Jack Hillers died in the fullness of his years, having lived a truly remarkable life. He was buried in the enlisted men's section of Arlington National Cemetery, not far from the officers' section wherein lie his compatriots, A. H. Thompson and John Wesley Powell.

112. Hickory Nut Gap, western North Carolina, 1894. National Archives photo no. 57-PS-198 (Geological Survey Collection).

113. Esmeralda Inn, Hickory Nut Gap, North Carolina, 1894. The Inn was built some time prior to 1894. It burned down in 1917 and was replaced by another that still stands. National Archives photo no. 57-PS-196 (Geological Survey Collection).

114. Ore pit at Cranberry Iron
Mine, North Carolina, 1894.
The mine was also known as
the Cranberry Ore Bank, located in Avery County, northwestern North Carolina. Iron
ore occurred as surficial de-
posits at the site. The deposit
was discovered in 1781 and
worked systematically after
1821, when a forge was built
there. Iron from the mine
supplied Confederate forces
during the Civil War, but the
mine's most active period of
utilization was from about
1865 to 1930. National Archives photo no. 57-PS-187
(Geological Survey
Collection).

115. *Typical Iron Furnace, Southeastern U.S.*, Cranberry Iron Mine, North Carolina, 1894. Photograph shows a small blast furnace and smelter, probably at the Cranberry Mine, typical of iron smelting facilities in the South late in the nineteenth century. National Archives photo no. 57-PS-173A (Geological Survey Collection).

116. *Typical Farm of Higher Class,* western North Carolina, 1894. The farm appears to have been recently cleared. Hillers's caption would seem to separate the farm from smaller farmsteads found throughout the Appalachian country. National Archives photo no. 57-PS-273 (Geological Survey Collection).

117. Tallulah Falls, Georgia, 1894. National Archives photo no. 57-PS-170 (Geological Survey Collection).

TALLULAH FALLS, GA.

Notes

1. J. W. Powell, "Report of the Director," *U.S. Geological Survey,* pp. xxxv–vi; W. H. Holmes, "Division of Illustrations," p. 97.

2. Viola, *Diplomats in Buckskins.*

3. Ewers, *Artists of the Old West,* pp. 10–22, 38–52; Viola, *Indian Legacy of Charles Bird King.* Many of the early portraits were reproduced in the magnificent color plates in McKenney and Hall, *History of the Indian Tribes of North America.* On the photographic portraits, see Glenn, "The 'Curious Gallery.'"

4. Scherer, *Indians,* pp. 151–52. Ross's 1858 portrait appears on p. 156.

5. Glenn, "The Curious Gallery," p. 249; Scherer, *Indians,* p. 152.

6. H. M. Teller, "Order," dated Jan. 28, 1884.

7. J. W. Powell, "Report of the Director," *Ninth Annual Report,* p. xli.

8. J. G. Morgan to J. W. Powell, Aug. 23, 1892 (Bureau of American Ethnology Correspondence). Beveridge's was initially a boarding house, and later the Washington House Hotel that catered to visiting Indian delegations for many years (Viola, *Diplomats in Buckskins*).

9. Since 1875, Hillers's Indian portraits have appeared in numerous government publications, and in privately printed books, monographs, and articles. No accurate count has been made, but an estimate would be several hundred.

10. Hillers Records.

11. Cline, *Exploring the Great Basin,* p. 175.

12. Huntington, *Yosemite Story,* pp. 9–12; Kroeber, *Handbook of the Indians of California,* p. 897.

13. Naef and Wood, *Era of Exploration, passim.*

14. Naef and Wood, *Era of Exploration,* p. 36, figs. 43–44.

15. Walcott, "Report of the Director," *Sixteenth Annual Report,* p. 79.

16. Sondley, *Hickory Nut Gorge,* p. 6; W. S. Powell, *North Carolina Gazetteer,* p. 224.

17. Sondley, *Hickory Nut Gorge,* pp. 6–7; J. A. Mobley and T. D. Burke, North Carolina Department of Cultural Resources, Raleigh, personal communication, Sept. 2 and 18, 1981.

18. Tallulah River and Falls were apparently named for an ancient Cherokee Indian settlement on the Tallulah River in Rabun County, Georgia, although the etymology of the term is uncertain (Hodge, *Handbook of American Indians* 2: 679).

The inimitable Tallulah Bankhead reported that she had been named for her paternal grandmother, who in turn had been named for the Falls. She thought that Tallulah may have been an Indian word of an "unidentified" tribe, and that the word meant either "love-maiden" or "Goddess of Vengeance." On the other hand, Ms. Bankhead wrote that an Irish poet once told her the name was derived from a sixth-century Irish saint and meant "colleen." Further, he said, the name was applied to the Falls by a group of "fugitive Hibernians [who] fled to Georgia long before Button Gwinnet signed the Declaration [of Independence]" (Tallulah Bankhead, *Tallulah,* pp. 23–24). With all due respect to the late Ms. Bankhead, and the Irish poet, we opt for the Cherokee derivation.

19. Walcott, "Report of the Director," *Seventeenth Annual Report,* p. 118, and *Nineteenth Annual Report,* pp. 140–41.

20. Walcott, "Report of the Director," *Twentieth Annual Report,* p. 160.

Hillers's Work in Retrospect

Sometime between his 1892 trip to Yosemite Valley and 1900 when he relinquished control of the Geological Survey photographic laboratory, Hillers looked over his accumulated life work and selected some sixty examples from the thousands of images he had taken. These he printed in an 11 × 14 inch format and put them together in an album. His choices included selections from his early work in and around Zion Canyon, the Grand Canyon, and southern Utah; from the Southwest he chose photographs from Hopi, Zuni, the Rio Grande pueblos, and Canyon de Chelly; finally he chose some of his Yosemite photographs. Several of the illustrations in this book (figs. 13, 56–60, 69, 72, 75, 107, 108) represent images he selected for this album. Other illustrations represent images he selected, but are not reproduced from his personally selected positives. He had an appreciation of his own work—as always, his eye was good.

Jack Hillers gave the world much more to appreciate than just the sixty photographs he chose for his own album. His photographic career was unique in many ways. His entire professional life was spent as a government photographer, working for federal agencies concerned with research; that is with the "increase and diffusion of knowledge among men," to quote the motto of the Smithsonian Institution. In that regard, Hillers was unique among nineteenth-century photographers. Jackson, O'Sullivan, Bell, and others worked for one or a few years for federal research organizations, but their careers cannot be seen in the same context as Hillers's career.

Because he worked solely for organizations dedicated to conveying information to various publics, Hillers's works probably were more widely disseminated, and seen by more people in the nineteenth century and since, than

any of his peers'. First, his photographs were used as the bases for engravings or woodcut illustrations, and later (as printing technology improved) for half tones, in many publications of the Bureau of American Ethnology and the Geological Survey. No actual count has been made of the number of Hillers's images used in those publications during his active career, but it would likely run to well over four hundred examples. Bureau of Ethnology and Geological Survey publications were widely distributed. Often as many as 10,000 copies were ordered printed. The volumes were distributed to scholars and libraries around the world, as well as to the American public through offices of Congressional delegates, and, by request, directly from the agencies to interested individuals. Hillers's photographs have been used in dozens of publications issued since 1900 by the Bureau of Ethnology and the National Museum of Natural History (both Smithsonian entities), as well as the Geological Survey and various other government agencies. Again, there is no actual count of how many have thus been used, but several hundred would be a fair estimate.

Since government photographs are in the public domain, and copies therefore are easily obtainable, Hillers's photographs have been used as illustrations in hundreds of university press and commercial press publications, magazines, and journals, as well as in museum exhibits at the Smithsonian and elsewhere, for a century. From the beginning his photographs were used to illustrate popular articles and books written by Powell, and later, articles and books by Hillers's great friend and river-running companion, Frederick S. Dellenbaugh.[1]

Thousands of copies of the stereographs that Hillers made from 1872 through at least 1879 were duplicated by the Jarvis Company of Washington, D.C., and other stereograph production companies, and sold to the public. Numerous sets also wound up in the parlors of congressmen and senators and their relatives in the 1870s—tokens of esteem from Powell at appropriations time.

Finally, Hillers's prints and transparencies were shown at several international expositions from 1876 to 1904. Following the Philadelphia Centennial celebration in 1876, a sort of "Exposition madness" gripped the United States and Europe. In the United States between 1883 and 1904 major expositions included the Southern Exposition in Louisville, Kentucky (1883), the Cotton Centennial Exposition in New Orleans (1884), the Cincinnati Exposition (1888), the Cotton States and International Exposition in Atlanta (1895), the Nashville Exposition (1897), the Omaha Exposition (1898), the Pan-American Exposition in Buffalo, New York (1901), the Charleston Exhibition (1901–02), and the Louisiana Purchase Exposition in St. Louis in 1904. In addition, there was the 1892 Columbian Historical Exposition in Madrid, and the tandem Chicago World's Columbian Exposition in 1893. There were also major expositions in Paris in 1878, 1889, and 1900, and in many other European cities as well.[2]

The Division of Ethnology of the U.S. National Museum, an entity of the Smithsonian, contributed exhibits to all of the American expositions listed above, and the Bureau of Ethnology and the Geological Survey to most of them.[3] Hillers's photographs and transparencies were displayed at most of these expositions, most notably at Madrid and Chicago in 1892–93, Atlanta in 1895, Buffalo in 1901, and St. Louis in 1904. At the latter two he received awards.

Hillers's work was prominently featured at Madrid and Chicago. A catalog in the Smithsonian National Anthropological Archives lists over forty large glass transparencies of American Indian portraits, pueblo villages, and southwestern archaeological sites sent to Madrid and subsequently to Chicago.[4] Based on the titles in the catalog, at least twenty-five of the transparencies were Hillers photographs, and he undoubtedly printed the remainder. In addition, there were over 1,300 photographs of American Indians exhibited at Madrid, although apparently fewer at Chicago. An official report on Madrid states: "*Photographs of Indians.* Representing 85 different tribes of the majority of stocks still in existence. This magnificent series of 1,300 photographs is the result of

the work of many years of collection by the U.S. Geological Survey and the Bureau of Ethnology. . . . The Bureau of Ethnology . . . exhibited their great map showing the distribution of the Indian linguistic stocks, upon which Major Powell and his assistants have been working assiduously for a number of years. This Bureau exhibited a large number of photographic transparencies of scenery, Indian villages, their inhabitants, etc., which adorned the windows of the halls and were greatly admired."[5]

It is not clear how many of the 1,300 photographs were actually mounted for display. Photographs of one of the Madrid exhibit halls show a number of large, framed photographs, spaced several feet apart, around the room. Beneath them is a row of contiguously mounted portraits, lithographs from the McKenney and Hall publication of 1826.[6] Probably the bulk of the photographs were available in albums.

At Chicago in 1893, in addition to Hillers's Indian photographs and transparencies, there were also a number of large glass transparencies of geological subjects, which Hillers and others had prepared. One of these was a 4 × 7 foot map of the United States, showing the location of oil fields and refineries. Others possibly included some of Hillers's Yosemite photographs. A photograph of the Smithsonian anthropology exhibit shows Powell's map, some transparencies, and a large number of framed photographs.[7] The attendance at the Madrid Exposition was apparently not large, although probably several thousand people saw the United States exhibits. Over seventeen million people thronged the Chicago Exposition in 1893 and presumably a large number of them saw the Smithsonian exhibits in the Government Building.

The large glass transparencies used at the various expositions were black and white. Color transparencies would have had a larger visual impact and Hillers became intrigued with their use for exhibit purposes. After 1900, "he experimented with non-fading water colors, protective coatings for colored transparencies, and collodion mixtures."[8] The Hillers family still possesses a number of these transparencies, some nearly three by four feet in size.

In the 1930s, Hillers's work began to attract the attention of historians of photography. Robert Taft's *Photography and the American Scene,* first published in 1938, kindled a renewed interest in (and became a baseline source for) the study of nineteenth-century American photography. The publication of Hillers's diary of the

1871–75 years helped continue interest in him, and it has been used in various recent histories of American photography.[9]

Hillers's work has been considered by art historians in relation to the luminist movement, a genre of painting and photography characterized by the brilliant use of atmospheric light and reflection, in the latter part of the nineteenth century.[10] It is not clear how much influence the works of luminist painters had on Hillers. He was certainly aware of the works of at least one landscape artist regarded as being on the edge of the movement, Albert Bierstadt.[11] Whatever influences art historians may discern in Hillers's work, it is clear that he had a great sense of composition and balance and the use of light and shadow. Like his peers, Jackson, O'Sullivan, Bell, Watkins, Muybridge, and other nineteenth-century "wet-plate artists," Jack Hillers took photography in America from mere recording to high art.

Hillers again differs from his contemporaries in that he was a government photographer, and that he worked for the same person, John Wesley Powell, for twenty-five years. Thus, his overall work and his choice of subject matter were determined by the interests, and research and exhibition needs, of Powell and the anthropologists and geologists around him. But Powell appreciated talent above all else, and, within the general framework of agreed-upon assignments, gave his scientific staff members great freedom to pursue their interests and express their abilities. Hillers enjoyed perhaps even more freedom, as Powell's 1883 letter to A. H. Thompson indicates: "Hillers may take pictures where he pleases until further orders."

Powell's and Hillers's long association and friendship endured until Powell's death in 1902. What began as a chance meeting bore great fruit, for Powell, for Hillers, and for the world at large. John Wesley Powell left the world a great scientific and organizational legacy. Jack Hillers, under Powell's comradely guidance, left the world a great visual legacy in his images of the West and Southwest, Oklahoma, the Southeast, and California, and his portraits of prominent American Indians. Thus the chance meeting in Salt Lake City has enriched the lives of many for over a century.

Notes

1. J. W. Powell, "Canons of the Colorado," "Overland Trip to Grand Canon," "Ancient Province of Tusayan," and *Exploration of the Colorado River;* Dellenbaugh, *Romance of the Colorado River* and *Canyon Voyage.*

2. Benedict, *Anthropology of World's Fairs,* table 3.

3. Hough, "Historical Sketch of the Division of Ethnology."

4. Mindeleff, "List of Transparencies."

5. Luce et al., *Report,* pp. 11–12, 213, and plates II-III.

6. Hough, "Columbian Historical Exposition," p. 271; McKenney, *History of the Indian Tribes of North America,* passim.

7. Fagin, "Closed Collections and Open Appeals," p. 254.

8. Darrah, "Beaman, Fennemore, Hillers," p. 497.

9. For example, Current, *Photography and the Old West;* Naef and Wood, *Era of Exploration;* National Archives and Records Service, *American Image;* Ostroff, *Western Views and Eastern Visions.*

10. Wilmerding, "Luminist Movement," pp. 102, 139–40.

11. Hillers, *Diary,* pp. 5, 115, and above, chapter 2.

Appendix:
A Note on Attribution

There are a variety of problems related to some of the photographs attributed to Jack Hillers. The following discussion is presented as an aid to future photohistorians. The principal sources of confusion are two. One is an inaccurate manuscript catalog, "Catalogue of Negatives, River, Land and Ethnographic, 1871-72-73-74-75-76," in the National Anthropological Archives, Smithsonian Institution. The second results from the way Hillers's and others' negatives and photographs were transferred from the U.S. Geological Survey to the Still Pictures Division of the National Archives and Records Service, apparently in the 1940s.

I. The 1870s Catalog

The "Catalogue of Negatives" was probably compiled by, or under the direction of, James C. Pilling, who was Powell's chief clerk for many years. The catalog is in at least three hands, one possibly Pilling's, the others those of copyists. John Wesley Powell was clearly involved in the compilation of the catalog to some extent, since some of its lists include many Southern Numic (Ute-Paiute) place names and names of objects. The catalog has fifteen separate sections labeled, variously, "river views," "land views," and "ethnographic," followed by "stereoscopic," "5 × 8," and "8 × 10." A sixteenth section of the catalog is undated. It is titled "Stereoscopic" and lists 174 stereographs of ethnographic and archaeological scenes taken between 1871 and 1879.

No. 1, "1871 River Views (Stereoscopic)" lists 132 stereographs made by, and attributed to, E. O. Beaman during the 1871 river trip from Green River City, Wyoming, to the Paria River.

No. 2, "1871 River Views 5 × 8" lists 32 photographs attributed to E. O. Beaman from Green River City to Bonita Bend in Labyrinth Canyon of the Green River.

No. 3, "1873 River Views, 5 × 8" lists 4 photographs in Glen Canyon attributed to James Fennemore. These were taken while the Canonita was being moved from the mouth of the Dirty Devil River to the Paria. It also lists 5 Grand Canyon photographs attributed to Hillers.

No. 4, "1872 River Views Stereographic" lists 45 stereographs grouped in a "Glen Canon series" and attributed to Fennemore. A "Marble Canon series" and a "Grand Canon series" list 41 stereographs made by Hillers during the August 1872 boat trip from Lee's Ferry to the mouth of Kanab Canyon.

Given the evidence from extant diaries, it is clear that all the attributions in Nos. 1-4 are correct.

No. 5, "1872 Land Views Stereoscopic" lists 20 "Views on Kolob Plateau" and 7 "Views on Uinkarets Mountains." These were initially attributed to Hillers, but his name is crossed out and Fennemore's written over it. Again from diary evidence, the attribution to Fennemore is correct. He was in charge and Hillers was assisting him when the photographs were taken.

No. 6, "1873 River Views, 5 × 8" lists 10 photographs of scenes along the North Rim of the Grand Canyon. These were probably taken in February 1873. Thompson, "Diary," p. 108 indicates that Hillers started from Kanab, Utah, to the North Rim on January 24 and returned on February 10, 1873, and that he had "got about a dozen views."

No. 7, "1873 River Views Stereoscopic—Grand Canon series" lists 17 stereographs, 7 of which match titles listed in No. 6. Some of the others could have been taken during the January-February 1873 trip. Others probably were taken in August 1873 during the trip with Moran and others to the North Rim. Hillers had a stereo camera with him at that time.

No. 8, "1873 Land Views Stereoscopic." (a) "Views on Kanab Creek." Thompson, "Diary," pp. 110-11 indicates that the 8 stereographs listed were made between June 24 and July 1, 1873. (b) "Views on Rio Virgin." This section lists negative numbers 9-33 and 49-53. These are stereographs of Parunuweap Canyon (the lower East Fork of the Virgin River) and the mouth of Zion Canyon ("Mukoontuweap," as Powell called it). They were taken during Hillers's trip to the area between April 4 and May

22, 1873 (Thompson, "Diary," pp. 109-10). (c) "Views on the Sevier River" lists 15 stereographs. These were made in both 1873 and 1875. Thompson, "Diary," pp. 111, 123 mentions Hillers photographing in the area in June 1873 and July 1875. (d) "Views on Kanab Creek" lists 26 stereographs. The majority of them were made in Lower Kanab Canyon in September 1872 at the end of the Grand Canyon river trip. Several are specifically mentioned by Hillers (*Diary*, pp. 142-44). A few were taken in Upper Kanab Canyon between February 18 and 25, 1873 (Thompson, "Diary," p. 108).

No. 9, "1873 Ethnographic Views, Stereoscopic." (a) "Kai-vav-its" [Kaibab Southern Paiute]. The list combines shots taken at Kanab, Utah, on October 4-5, 1872 (W. C. Powell, "Journal," pp. 457-58) and those from August 1873 when Hillers was assisted by Thomas Moran in "posing" the Indians. Stereograph 38, "Waiting for the kettle to boil," is attributed to E. O. Beaman but the name is crossed out and Hillers's substituted. This may be the single ethnographic photograph Beaman reports he was able to make in January 1872 ("The Canons of the Colorado and the Moqui Pueblos," p. 457). The same 40 Kaibab stereographs are listed in the undated section 16 of the catalog (see below). (b) "U-ai-Nu-ints" lists 11 stereographs of Southern Paiutes around St. George, Utah. They were taken by Hillers in late August 1873 during the Powell-Ingalls trip to that area. (c) "Mo-a-pa-ri-ats" [Moapa Southern Paiute] lists 9 stereographs taken by Hillers in early September 1873 in the Moapa Valley, Nevada, during the Powell-Ingalls inquiry. (d) "Nu-a-gun-tits" [Las Vegas Southern Paiute] lists 14 stereographs taken by Hillers in September 1873 at Las Vegas, Nevada. (e) "Uintah Utes" [Utes of Uintah Basin, Utah]. See discussion in No. 10, below. (f) "Nav-a-jos" lists 2 stereographs attributed to Beaman, but his name is scratched out and Hillers's written above. Hillers (*Diary*, p. 149) and Clem Powell ("Journal," p. 460) mention encounters with Navajos on the way to the Hopi pueblos in 1872, but not photographing them. The attribution remains uncertain. They may have been made by Beaman during his trip to Hopi in early 1872 and later found their way into the Powell collection. (g) "Shi-nu-mos" [Hopi] lists 6 stereographs attributed to Hillers. These may derive from the ill-fated October 1872 trip to Hopi described in chapter 2, although the results from that trip were apparently extremely poor. They may alternatively derive from Hillers's January 1876 trip to Hopi noted in Chapter 3. (h) No title. Lists 3 views of "Ancient Ruins on the Cliffs of Glen Canon." These are attributed to Fennemore, but his name is then scratched out and Hillers's name added. These were taken by Fennemore on June 26, 1872, during the boat trip through Glen Canyon from the Dirty Devil River to the Paria River (Hillers, *Diary*, p. 125 and fig. 6).

No. 10, "1874 Ethnographic Views, Stereographic" lists 29 stereographs of Uintah Utes, all attributed to Hillers. These have been carefully scrutinized by Fleming and Luskey (*North American*

Indians, passim) and Lessard ("E. O. Who?"). It is clear from the Powell expedition diaries and Beaman's own publications (see bibliography) that Beaman took a number of photographs of Utes in 1871 while the river party paused in the Uintah Basin (see chapter 1, above). The 3 photographs of Utes used in this book (figs. 30-32) are attributed to Hillers in 1874 with some certainty. *The Mirror Case* has Powell in the picture. The only time Powell could have been with the Utes when a camera was present was in 1874. The other two, *Antero* and *Pah-ri-ats*, appear to have the same grove of trees in the background. All other Uintah Ute photographs attributed to Hillers are problematic. At least 4 listed by Lessard are clearly by Beaman, although probably not *Pah-ri-ats*.

No. 11, "1874 River Views 8 × 10" lists 7 views of Flaming Gorge, the Gate of Ladore, and other places in the Green River area and the Uintah Valley. These are attributed to Hillers and apparently derive from the 1874 trip.

No. 12, "1874 River Views Stereographic" lists 13 shots, duplicating some in No. 11. These are photographs taken along Vermillion, Ashley, and Brush creeks, all tributaries of the upper Green River, taken during the 1874 trip.

No. 13, "1875 Land Views 8 × 10" lists 16 views taken during the 1875 field trip Hillers made with A. H. Thompson and G. K. Gilbert in southern Utah.

No. 14, "1875 Land Views, Stereoscopic" lists 84 stereographs taken during the 1875 field season in southern Utah.

No. 15, "1875 Ethnographic Views 8 × 10" lists 9 of the portraits of Plains Indians made at Okmulgee, Indian Territory, May 10-12, 1875 (Hillers, *Diary*, p. 158).

No. 16, "Stereoscopic." This is an undated list of 174 stereographs of Paiutes, Utes, Navajos, Hopis, Glen Canyon ruins, the 9 Plains Indians of No. 15, Zuni, and two ruins in Canyon de Chelly, Arizona. It would have to have been compiled after 1879.

II. The National Archives Catalog

The Hillers photographs on deposit in the Still Pictures Division of the National Archives and Records Service in Washington, D.C. (Record Group 57-PS) are listed in a manuscript catalog compiled in 1967 and 1968 by Nellie C. Carico, then of the Topographic Division of the U.S. Geological Survey: "List of the Hiller [sic] Photographic Albums I, II, III, IV and V of the Powell Survey." The albums have an obviously long, but quite unclear history. The albums and many negatives were turned over to the National Archives some time after 1948. Prior to that time, many of the original glass negatives were "Destroyed by authority of the Administrative Geologist," one Dr. Julian D. Sears. The numbering within the albums is not consistent, and this inconsistency is reflected in the listings given below. Where other photographers are known, or are listed in the albums, the names are given. The corrections are based on information derived from U.S. Geological Survey *Annual Reports,* and from the Powell Survey correspondence and Bureau of American Ethnology correspondence.

Album I.

Nos. 1-27. Charleston, South Carolina, after the earthquake of August 31, 1886. C. C. Jones photographs.

28-52. Yosemite Valley region, California. Hillers, 1892.

53. Yosemite Valley. "Photography by Fiske," no date.

54-60, 66, 68-69. Niagara Falls. Photographer(s) and dates unknown.

61-63. Grand Canyon. Hillers, August 1873.

64. Zion Canyon. Hillers, 1873.

78. Monroe Canyon, Utah. Hillers, probably 1873.

Album II.

66, 68. Grand Canyon. Hillers, 1873.

69-70, 85-86. Ladore Canyon. E. O. Beaman, 1871.

71. Marble Pinnacle, Kanab Canyon. Hillers, 1872.

72, 79. Grand Canyon. Hillers, 1873.

73-78, 80-81, 95. Virgin River area, Utah. Hillers, 1873.

97-100, 105, 108, 110. Bullion Canyon area, Utah. Hillers, probably 1873.

83. Gate of Ladore, Green River, Utah, J. C. Pilling in photograph. Hillers, 1874.

84-95. Canyon de Chelly, Arizona. Hillers, 1879-82.

96-101, 112-113, 142. Fort Wingate area, New Mexico. Hillers, 1883.

102-106. Flagstaff area, Arizona. Hillers, 1885.

107. Johnson Canyon, Santa Fe Railroad. Possibly by Hillers; date unknown.

108. Chihuahua, Mexico. Photographer and date unknown.

109-110. Canyon Diablo, Arizona. Hillers, 1883.

111. Shinarump Cliff, Escalante River, Utah. Hillers, 1875.

113-122. Northern Florida. Hillers, 1894.

123-126. Yellowstone National Park area. C. D. Walcott, no date.

Album III.

127-163. Yellowstone National Park area. Possibly by C. D. Walcott; dates unknown.

164-185. Southeastern United States. Hillers, 1894.

Album IV. (Duplicates from Album II not repeated.)

190-217, 300-302, 305, 306, 309. Southeastern United States. Hillers, 1894.

218-244. Geology shots in vicinity of Washington, D.C. Hillers, 1880s-90s.

247-254, 363. Photographs of wax geological models. Presumably photographed by Hillers; dates unknown.

418-425, 757, 763. Aquarius Plateau area, Utah. Hillers, 1875.

426-430, 439, 461, 471-473, 476, 479-487, 506, 508-510, 512, 518. Green River areas, Wyoming and Utah. E. O. Beaman, 1871.

432, 475. Glen Canyon. Probably by E. O. Beaman, 1871.

440-441, 453-455, 464, 465-469, 507. Kanab area, Utah. Hillers, 1873.

444, 506. Start of second river trip, Green River City, Wyoming Territory. E. O. Beaman, May 1871.

448. Aquarius Plateau, Utah. Hillers, 1872.

450, 458. Grand Canyon area. Hillers, 1873.

462-463. Keam's Canyon Trading Post, Arizona. Hillers, probably 1879.

488-499, 505. Green River area, Wyoming and Utah. Hillers, 1874.

Album V. (Duplicates from Album IV not repeated.)

401-417. Wax geological models by Willis Bailey, 1891. Presumably photographed by Hillers; dates unknown.

418-425, 683. Aquarius Plateau–Henry Mountain area, Utah. Hillers, 1872, 1875.

426, 487-488. Tower on Vermillion Creek, Brown's Park, Green River area. Hillers, 1874.

427-429, 459. Green River area, Wyoming. E. O. Beaman, 1871.

430. Brown's Park, Green River area. Attributed to Beaman, but may be by another unknown photographer; date unknown.

431, 431-A, 433-438, 458, 693. Grand Canyon area. Hillers, 1873.

439. Ashley Falls, Green River. E. O. Beaman, 1871.

440-441. Kanab area, Utah. Hillers, 1873.

442. Bullion Canyon, Utah. Hillers, 1873.

444, 506, 506-A. Start of second river trip, Green River Station, Wyoming. E. O. Beaman, May 1871.

448, 526. Aquarius Plateau, Bee Lake, Utah. Hillers, 1872.

449. Sockdologer Rapid, Grand Canyon. Possibly by Hillers, 1872.

450. Mt. Trumbull region, Arizona. Hillers, 1873.

451. Grand Canyon. Hillers, 1873.

452, 461, 744, 749, 751. Desolation Canyon, Green River, Utah. E. O. Beaman, 1871.

453-456, 464, 466-469, 507, 513, 516, 624. Kanab area, Utah. Hillers, 1873.

457. Possibly Bullion Canyon, Utah. Hillers, 1873.

460. Unidentified landscape. Photographer and date unknown.

462-463. Keam's Canyon, Arizona. Hillers, 1879 or later.

465. Pilling's Cascade, Utah. Hillers, 1873.

471-473, 476-478, 480-485. Green River area. E. O. Beaman, 1871.

486-495. Green River area. Hillers, 1874.

496-501, 508-510, 512, 517-518, 521-522, 524, 527-528, 534, 536, 538-539, 545, 551, 554-556, 559, 561-566, 571, 575, 577, 580-581, 584-585, 588, 590, 593, 599-601, 603-605, 608, 610, 612, 620-621, 626, 628, 630, 642, 645, 649, 657, 662, 669, 671-672, 674, 677, 680-681, 684. Green River area. E. O. Beaman, 1871.

502-505, 687. Green River area. Hillers, 1874.

511, 515, 557, 574, 598, 602, 615-616, 618, 623, 627. Grand Canyon area. Hillers, 1873.

519. Jack Hillers on talus slope with two horses. Probably by A. H. Thompson, 1872.

520, 523, 530, 532, 535, 537, 541-542, 547, 549, 586, 591, 594, 607, 614, 617, 631, 641, 643, 654, 663-664, 703, 712. Virgin River area, Utah. Hillers, 1873.

525. Head of Paria River—Hogbacks. Photographer and date unknown.

552, 566, 578, 606, 613, 619, 622, 625, 629, 632, 634, 636, 638, 640, 644, 647, 650-651, 656, 659, 667-668, 673, 675, 679, 682, 685, 688, 692. Lower Kanab Canyon, Arizona. Hillers, 1872.

569. Glen Canyon (?), John Steward in photograph. E. O. Beaman, 1871.

583, 589, 670. Escalante River area, southern Utah. Hillers, 1872 or 1875.

596, 689, 697, 701, 706, 709, 717. Kolob Plateau, Utah. J. Fennemore, 1872.

633, 661. A. H. Thompson and his horse "Old Ute." Hillers, 1872.

653, 711, 735, 738. Glen Canyon. J. Fennemore, 1872.

690, 694, 698, 700, 702. Green River—Split Mountain Canyon. E. O. Beaman, 1871.

704. Green River, cabin at "Fort Robidoux," with crew of 1871 river trip in photograph. E. O. Beaman, 1871. (See Dellenbaugh, *Romance of the Colorado River,* p. 264.)

707-708, 722-723, 727, 730, 733-734, 736. Green River, Labyrinth Canyon. E. O. Beaman, 1871.

710. Colorado River, ruin opposite the mouth of the Dirty Devil River. J. Fennemore, 1872. (See Hillers, *Diary,* fig. 6.)

713-714, 716, 719. Green River, Desolation Canyon, Utah. E. O. Beaman, 1871.

724. Tantalus Creek, Henry Mountains, Utah. Hillers, 1875.

737. Mt. Post, Colorado. W. H. Jackson, 1870.

739, 741, 743. Bonito Bend, Green River, Utah. E. O. Beaman, 1871.

747. Junction of Grand and Green rivers, at top of cliffs. E. O. Beaman, 1871.

748. Colorado River, head of Cataract Canyon, Utah. E. O. Beaman, 1871.

753, 754, 758, 764. Colorado River, Cataract Canyon, Utah. E. O. Beaman, 1871.

762, 768. Spring Creek, Fish Lake Mountain, Utah. Hillers, 1873.

766. Grand Canyon. Confluence of Colorado and Little Colorado rivers. Hillers, 1872.

767, 770, 775, 780, 783, 785, 789-792, 799, 800, 803. Glen Canyon, Utah. Either Beaman, 1871, or Fennemore, 1872.

769. Colorado River—boats of Powell Expedition. E. O. Beaman, 1871.

771. Ward's Cascade, Nettle Creek, Utah. Hillers, 1875.

772, 773, 776, 777, 781-782, 786, 805, 811, 822, 825, 829, 832. Aquarius Plateau area, Utah. Hillers, 1875.

778. Repairing boats at mouth of Dirty Devil River. J. Fennemore, 1872.

796. In Glen Canyon, "Music Temple." J. Fennemore, 1872.

804, 806, 808, 810, 812, 824, 827-828, 833-840. Glen Canyon, Colorado River. J. Fennemore, 1872.

807. Aspen Lake, Aquarius Plateau, Utah. Hillers, 1872.

809. J. K. Hillers at work on Aquarius Plateau, Utah. Probably by A. H. Thompson or G. K. Gilbert, 1875.

813. Pilling's Cascade, Utah. Hillers, 1873.

820, 845-846, 849-850, 854, 858. Marble Canyon, Colorado River. Hillers, 1872.

830. San Francisco Mountains, Arizona. Hillers, 1885.

841. "This is Hillers' white mule," Utah. Hillers, 1872-75.

842. Navajo Mountain from Aquarius Plateau. Hillers, 1872.

843, 844. Temple Creek, Aquarius Plateau, Utah. Hillers, 1875.

847-848, 851-853. Waterpocket Creek, Waterpocket Fold area, Utah. Hillers, 1875.

856. Green River Canyon, Utah; Powell's armchair boat. E. O. Beaman, 1871.

859-865, 867-868, 870, 873-874, 878, 880-884, 890, 907. Tantalus Creek, Henry Mountains area, Utah. Hillers, 1875.

866, 869, 871-872, 875-876, 879, 885, 888, 891-897, 899-906. Grand Canyon during 1872 river trip. Hillers, 1872.

908. Flaming Gorge, Green River, Wyoming. E. O. Beaman, 1871.

909. Ogden Canyon, Utah. W. H. Jackson, 1871.

910. Probably Garden of the Gods, Colorado. W. H. Jackson, about 1871.

Bibliography

Alinder, James, ed. *Carleton E. Watkins: Photographs of the Columbia River and Oregon.* The Friends of Photography, Carmel, Calif., 1979.

Alwood, John. *The Great Exhibitions.* Studio Vista, London, 1977.

Ambler, J. Richard. *The Anasazi.* Museum of Northern Arizona, Flagstaff, 1977.

Auer, Michael. *The Illustrated History of the Camera from 1839 to the Present.* New York Graphic Society, Boston, 1975.

Bailey, Paul D. *Jacob Hamblin, Buckskin Apostle.* Westernlore Press, Los Angeles, 1948.

Baird, Spencer F. "International Centennial Exhibition." In *Smithsonian Institution Annual Report for 1875,* pp. 58-71. Washington, 1876.

Bandelier, Adolph F. *The Southwestern Journal of Adolph F. Bandelier, 1880-1882.* Ed. Charles H. Lange and Carroll L. Riley. University of New Mexico Press, Albuquerque, 1966.

Bankhead, Tallulah. *Tallulah: My Autobiography.* Harper and Row, New York, 1952.

Bartlett, Richard H. *Great Surveys of the American West.* University of Oklahoma Press, Norman, 1962.

Bassford, Amy O., and Fritiof Fryxell, eds. *Home-Thoughts from Afar: Letters of Thomas Moran to Mary Nimmo Moran.* East Hampton Free Library, East Hampton, N.Y., 1967.

Basso, Keith H. "History of Ethnological Research." In Sturtevant, *Handbook of North American Indians* 9: 14-21.

Beaman, E. O. "Among the Aztecs." *Anthony's Photographic Bulletin* 3 (1872): 746-47.

———. "The Canons of the Colorado and the Moqui Pueblos." *Appleton's Journal* 11 (1874): 481-84, 513-16, 545-48, 590-93, 623-26, 641-44, 686, 689.

———. "The Colorado Exploring Expedition." *Anthony's Photographic Bulletin* 3 (1872): 463-65.

———. "A Tour through the Grand Canon of the Colorado." *Anthony's Photographic Bulletin* 3 (1872): 703-5.

Beaton, Cecil, and Gail Buckland. *The Magic Image: The Genius of Photography from 1839 to the Present Day.* Little, Brown, Boston, 1975.

Bender, Norman J. *Missionaries, Outlaws, and Indians: Taylor F. Ealey at Lincoln and Zuni, 1878-1881.* University of New Mexico Press, Albuquerque, 1984.

Benedict, Burton. *The Anthropology of World's Fairs: San Francisco's Panama Pacific International Exposition of 1915.* Lowie Museum of Anthropology, Berkeley, and Scolar Press, London, 1983.

Bourke, John Gregory. *The Snake Dance of the Moqui Indians of Arizona.* Scribner's, New York, 1884.

Braff, Phyllis. *Thomas Moran: A Search for the Scenic.* Guild Hall Museum, East Hampton, N.Y., 1980.

Brandes, Raymond S. "Frank Hamilton Cushing: Pioneer Americanist." Ph.D. dissertation, University of Arizona, Tucson, 1965.

Brew, J. O. "Hopi Prehistory and History to 1850." In Sturtevant, *Handbook of North American Indians* 9: 514-23.

Brooks, Juanita. *John Doyle Lee: Zealot-Pioneer Builder-Scapegoat.* Arthur H. Clarke Co., Glendale, 1972.

Bureau of American Ethnology Correspondence. Correspondence, Bureau of American Ethnology Collection, Smithsonian National Anthropological Archives, Washington, 1879-1910.

Casagrande, Louis B., and Phillips Bourns. *Side Trips: The Photography of Sumner W. Matteson, 1898-1908.* Milwaukee Public Museum, Milwaukee, and Science Museum of Minnesota, St. Paul, 1983.

Cline, Gloria Griffin. *Exploring the Great Basin.* University of Oklahoma Press, Norman, 1963.

Colburn, J. E. "The Colorado Canyon." *New York Times,* Aug. 13, 1873, p. 2.

———. "The Land of Mormon." *New York Times,* Aug. 7, 1873, p. 2.

Crampton, C. Gregory. *The Zunis of Cibola.* University of Utah Press, Salt Lake City, 1977.

Crawford, William. *The Keepers of Light: A History and Working Guide to Early Photographic Processes*. Morgan and Morgan, Dobbs Ferry, N.Y., 1979.

Current, Karen. *Photography and the Old West*. Harry Abrams, New York, 1978.

Cushing, Frank Hamilton. *My Life in Zuni*. American West Publishing Co., Palo Alto, 1970.

Darrah, William Culp. "Beaman, Fennemore, Hillers, Dellenbaugh, Johnson and Hattan." *Utah Historical Quarterly* 16-17 (1948-49): 495-97.

———. *Powell of the Colorado*. Princeton University Press, Princeton, N.J., 1954.

———. *The World of Stereographs*. Privately printed, Gettysburg, Pa., 1977.

Darrah, William Culp, ed. "Biographical Sketches and Original Documents of the First Powell Expedition of 1869." *Utah Historical Quarterly* 15 (1947): 1-148.

Dellenbaugh, Frederick S. *A Canyon Voyage: The Narrative of the Second Powell Expedition down the Green-Colorado River from Wyoming, and the Exploration on Land, in the Years 1871 and 1872*. G. P. Putnam's Sons, New York, 1908. Rpt. Yale University Press, New Haven, 1926, 1962.

———. *The Romance of the Colorado River: The Story of Its Discovery in 1540, with an Account of the Later Explorations, and with Special Reference to the Voyages of Powell through the Line of the Grand Canyons*. G. P. Putnam's Sons, New York, 1902.

Dingus, Rick. *The Photographic Artifacts of Timothy O'Sullivan*. University of New Mexico Press, Albuquerque, 1982.

Dutton, Clarence E. *Tertiary History of the Grand Canyon District*. U.S. Geological Survey Monograph, no. 2. Washington, 1882.

Earle, Edward W., ed. *Points of View: The Stereograph in America—A Cultural History*. Visual Studies Workshop Press, Rochester, N.Y., 1979.

Euler, Robert C. *Southern Paiute Ethnohistory*. University of Utah Anthropological Papers, no. 78. Salt Lake City, 1966.

Ewers, John C. *Artists of the Old West*. Doubleday and Co., Garden City, N.Y., 1965.

———. "Fact and Fiction in the Documentary History of the American West." In J. F. McDermott, ed., *The Frontier Reexamined*, pp. 79-95. University of Illinois Press, Urbana, 1967.

Fagin, Nancy L. "Closed Collections and Open Appeals: The Two Anthropology Exhibits at the Chicago World's Columbian Exposition of 1893." *Curator* 27 (1984): 249-64.

Flack, J. Kirkpatrick. *Desideratum in Washington: The Intellectual Community in the Capital City, 1870-1900*. Schenckman Publishing Co., Cambridge, Mass., 1975.

Fleming, Paula R., and Judith Luskey. *The North American Indians in Early Photographs*. Harper and Row, New York, 1986.

Foote, Shelby. *The Civil War, a Narrative: Red River to Appomattox*. Random House, New York, 1974.

Foreman, Grant. *Indian Removal: The Emigration of the Five Civilized Tribes*. University of Oklahoma Press, Norman, 1932.

Fowler, Don D., Robert C. Euler, and Catherine S. Fowler. *John Wesley Powell and the Anthropology of the Canyon Country*. U.S. Geological Survey Professional Paper, no. 670. Washington, 1969.

Fowler, Don D., and Catherine S. Fowler. "John Wesley Powell, Anthropologist." *Utah Historical Quarterly* 39 (1969): 152-72.

Fowler, Don D., and Catherine S. Fowler, eds. *Anthropology of the Numa: John Wesley Powell's Manuscripts on the Numic Peoples of Western North America, 1868-1880*. Smithsonian Contributions to Anthropology, no. 14. Washington, 1971.

———. "John Wesley Powell's Journal: Colorado River Explorations, 1871-1872." *Smithsonian Journal of History* 3 (1968): 1-44.

Fowler, Don D., and John F. Matley. *Material Culture of the Numa: The John Wesley Powell Collection, 1867-1880*. Smithsonian Contributions to Anthropology, no. 26. Washington, 1979.

Frazer, Robert W. *Forts of the West*. University of Oklahoma Press, Norman, 1965.

Frigout, Arlette. "Hopi Ceremonial Organization." In Sturtevant, *Handbook of North American Indians* 9: 564-76.

Gaede, Marnie, ed. *Camera, Spade and Pen: An Inside View of Southwestern Archaeology*. University of Arizona Press, Tucson, 1980.

Gernsheim, Helmut. *The Origins of Photography*. Thames and Hudson, London and New York, 1982.

Gilbert, George. *Photography: The Early Years. A Historical Guide for Collectors*. Harper and Row, New York, 1980.

Gilbert, Grove Karl. *Report on the Geology of the Henry Mountains*. Government Printing Office, Washington, 1877.

———. *Lake Bonneville*. U.S. Geological Survey Monograph, no. 1. Washington, 1890.

Glenn, James R. "The 'Curious Gallery': The Indian Photographs of the McClees Studio in Washington, 1857-1858." *History of Photography, an International Quarterly*, July 1981, pp. 249-62.

Goetzmann, William H. *Army Exploration in the American West, 1803-1863*. Yale University Press, New Haven, 1959.

———. *Exploration and Empire: The Explorer and the Scientist in the Winning of the American West*. Alfred A. Knopf, New York, 1966.

Gregory, H. E., W. C. Darrah, and C. Kelly, eds. "The Exploration of the Colorado River and the High Plateaus of Utah by the Second Powell Expedition of 1871-72." *Utah Historical Quarterly* 16-17 (1948-49): 1-540.

Grinnell, George B. *The Fighting Cheyennes*. Charles Scribner's Sons, New York, 1915. Rpt. University of Oklahoma Press, Norman, 1956.

Hillers, John K. *"Photographed All the Best Scenery": Jack Hillers's Diary of the Powell Expedition, 1871-1875.* Ed. Don D. Fowler. University of Utah Press, Salt Lake City, 1972.

Hillers Records.
Service K3 and L4 U.S. Art. Date of Filing 1891, Feb. 6, app. #987089, cert #735701, D.C. U.S. National Archives and Records Service, Washington, D.C.

Hine, Robert V. *In the Shadow of Fremont: Edward Kern and the Art of American Exploration, 1845-1860.* University of Oklahoma Press, Norman, 1981.

Hinsley, Curtis M., Jr. "Ethnographic Charisma and Scientific Routine: Cushing and Fewkes in the American Southwest, 1879-1893." In G. W. Stocking, ed., *Observers Observed: Essays on Ethnographic Fieldwork,* pp. 53-69 History of Anthropology, vol. 1. University of Wisconsin Press, Madison, 1983.

———. *Savages and Scientists: The Smithsonian Institution and the Development of American Anthropology, 1846-1910.* Smithsonian Institution Press, Washington, 1981.

Hodge, Frederick Webb, ed. *Handbook of American Indians North of Mexico.* Bureau of American Ethnology Bulletin 30, pts. 1-2. Washington, 1907-10.

Holmes, Oliver Wendell. "Doings of the Sunbeam." *Atlantic Monthly* 12 (1863): 1-15.

———. "The Stereoscope and Stereograph." *Atlantic Monthly* 3 (1859): 738-48.

Holmes, William Henry. "The Division of Illustrations." *U.S. Geological Survey, Sixth Annual Report,* p. 97. Washington, 1885.

———. "A Note on the Ancient Remains of Southwestern Colorado Examined During the Summer of 1875." *Bulletin of the United States Geological and Geographical Survey of the Territories* 2, no. 1, pp. 3-24. Washington, 1876.

Horan, James D. *Mathew Brady: Historian with a Camera.* Crown Publishers, New York, 1955.

———. *Timothy O'Sullivan: America's Forgotten Photographer.* Bonanza Books, New York, 1966.

Hough, Walter. "The Columbian Historical Exposition in Madrid." *American Anthropologist,* o.s. 6 (1893): 271-77.

———. "Historical Sketch of the Division of Ethnology." 1906. Manuscript on file, Smithsonian National Anthropological Archives, Washington.

Huntington, Harriet E. *The Yosemite Story.* Doubleday and Co., Garden City, New York, 1966.

Ingram, J. S. *The Centennial Exhibition Described and Illustrated.* Hubbard Brothers, Philadelphia, 1876.

Jackson, Clarence S. *Picture Maker of the Old West: William Henry Jackson.* Charles Scribner's Sons, New York, 1947.

Jackson, William H. "Ancient Ruins in Southwestern Colorado." *Bulletin of the United States Geological and Geographical Survey of the Territories,* no. 1, pp. 17-30. Washington, 1875.

———. *The Diaries of W. H. Jackson, Frontier Photographer.* Ed.

Leroy R. Hafen and Ann W. Hafen. Arthur H. Clark Co., Glendale, 1959.

———. "A Notice of Ancient Ruins in Arizona and Utah Lying about the Rio San Juan." *Bulletin of the United States Geological and Geographical Survey of the Territories* 2, no. 2, pp. 25-45. Washington, 1876.

———. *The Pioneer Photographer: Rocky Mountain Adventure with a Camera.* World Book Co., Yonkers-on-Hudson, New York, 1929.

———. *Time Exposure: The Autobiography of William Henry Jackson.* G. P. Putnam's Sons, New York, 1940.

Johnson, Robert U., and Clarence C. Buel. *Battles and Leaders of the Civil War.* 4 vols. Thomas Yoseloff, New York and London, 1965.

Judd, Neil M. *The Bureau of American Ethnology, a Partial History.* University of Oklahoma Press, Norman, 1967.

Kennard, Edward A. *Hopi Kachinas.* 2d rev. ed. Museum of the American Indian, New York, 1970.

Kessell, John L. *Kiva, Cross and Crown: The Pecos Indians and New Mexico, 1540-1840.* National Park Service, Washington, 1979.

Kroeber, Alfred L. *Handbook of the Indians of California.* Bureau of American Ethnology Bulletin 78. Washington, 1925.

Lamar, Howard R. *The Far Southwest, 1846-1912: A Territorial History.* Yale University Press, New Haven, 1966.

Lessard, F. Dennis. "E. O. Who?" *American Indian Art Magazine* 12, no. 2 (1987): 52-61.

Lindstrom, Gaell. *Thomas Moran in Utah.* Utah State University, Special Publication, Logan, n.d.

Lockhurst, Kenneth W. *The Story of Exhibitions.* The Studio Publications, London and New York, 1951.

Long, E. B., and Barbara Long. *The Civil War Day by Day: An Almanac, 1861-1865.* Doubleday, Garden City, N.Y., 1971.

Luce, Stephen B., et al. *Report of the U.S. Commission to the Columbian Historical Exposition at Madrid, 1892-93.* Government Printing Office, Washington, 1895.

Maass, John. *The Glorious Enterprise: The Centennial Exhibition of 1876.* American Life Foundation, Watkins Glen, N.Y., 1973.

McCullough, Edo. *World's Fair Midways.* Arno Press, New York, 1966.

McKenney, Thomas, and James Hall. *History of the Indian Tribes of North America, with Biographical Sketches and Anecdotes of the Principal Chiefs.* 3 vols. F. W. Greenough, Philadelphia, 1836-44.

Malouf, C., and A. A. Malouf. "The Effects of Spanish Slavery on the Indians of the Intermountain West." *Southwestern Journal of Anthropology* 1 (1945): 378-91.

Mark, Joan. *Four Anthropologists: An American Science in Its Early Years.* Science History Publications, New York, 1980.

Marston, O. Dock. "The Lost Journal of John Colton Sumner." *Utah Historical Quarterly* 37 (1969): 73-89.

Mindeleff, Cosmos. "Catalogue of the Exhibits of the U.S. Geological Survey and the Bureau of Ethnology at the New Orleans Exposition." 1895. Manuscript on file, Smithsonian National Anthropological Archives, Washington.

———. "List of Transparencies . . . Available for Madrid and Chicago." 1892. Manuscript on file, Smithsonian National Anthropological Archives, Washington.

Möllhausen, Balduin. *Diary of a Journey from the Mississippi to the Coast of the Pacific with a U.S. Government Expedition.* 2 vols. Longman, Brown, Longmans and Roberts, London, 1858. Rpt. Johnson Reprint Corp., New York, 1969.

Naef, Weston J., and James N. Wood. *Era of Exploration: The Rise of Landscape Photography in the American West, 1860-1885.* New York Graphic Society, Boston, 1975.

National Archives and Records Service. *The American Image: Photographs from the National Archives, 1860-1960.* Pantheon Books, New York, 1979.

Newhall, Beaumont. *The Daguerreotype in America.* 3d rev. ed. Dover Publications, New York, 1976.

———. *The History of Photography from 1839 to the Present.* New York Graphic Society, Boston, 1982.

Newhall, Beaumont, and Diana E. Edkins. *William H. Jackson.* Morgan and Morgan, Dobbs Ferry, N.Y., 1974.

Newhall, Beaumont, and Nancy Newhall. *T. H. O'Sullivan, Photographer.* Eastman House, Rochester, N.Y., and Amon Carter Museum, Fort Worth, 1966.

Ostroff, Eugene. *Western Views and Eastern Visions.* Smithsonian Institution Traveling Exhibition Service and the U.S. Geological Survey, Washington, 1981.

Packhard, Gar, and Maggy Packhard. *Southwest 1880 with Ben Wittick, Pioneer Photographer.* Packhard Publications, Santa Fe, 1970.

Palmer, William J. *Report of Surveys across the Continent, in 1867-68 on the 35th and 32nd Parallels for a Route Extending the Kansas Pacific Railway to the Pacific Ocean.* Selheimer Printer, Philadelphia, 1869.

Palmquist, Peter E. *Carleton E. Watkins, Photographer of the American West.* University of New Mexico Press, Albuquerque, and Amon Carter Museum, Fort Worth, 1982.

Pollack, Peter. *The Picture History of Photography from the Earliest Beginnings to the Present Day.* Harry Abrams, New York, 1969.

Porter, Eliot. *The Place No One Knew: Glen Canyon on the Colorado.* Sierra Club-Ballentine Books, New York, 1968.

Powell, John Wesley. "The Ancient Province of Tusayan." *Scribner's Monthly* 11 (1875): 193-213.

———. "The Cañons of the Colorado." *Scribner's Monthly* 9 (1875): 293-310, 523-37.

———. "Chuar's Illusion." *Science* 3 (1896): 263-71.

———. *Down the Colorado: Diary of the First Trip through the Grand Canyon, 1869.* Ed. Don D. Fowler; epilogue and pho-tographs by Eliot Porter. E. P. Dutton, New York, 1969.

———. *The Exploration of the Colorado River of the West and Its Tributaries; Explored in 1869, 1870, 1871 and 1872, under the Direction of the Secretary of the Smithsonian Institution.* Government Printing Office, Washington, 1875. Rpt. as Powell, *Down the Colorado.*

———. "An Overland Trip to the Grand Cañon." *Scribner's Monthly* 10 (1875) 659-78.

———. "Report of the Director." In *First Annual Report of the Bureau of Ethnology, 1879-1880,* pp. xi-xxxiii. Washington, 1881.

———. "Report of the Director." In *Ninth Annual Report of the Bureau of Ethnology, 1887-1888,* pp. xxiii-xlvi. Washington, 1892.

———. "Report of the Director." In *U.S. Geological Survey, Fifth Annual Report,* pp. ix-xli. Washington, 1885.

———. *Report on the Geology of the Eastern Portion of the Uintah Mountains and a Region of the Country Adjacent Thereto, with Atlas.* Government Printing Office, Washington, 1876.

———. *Report on the Lands of the Arid Region of the United States, with a More Detailed Account of the Lands of Utah.* Government Printing Office, Washington, 1878.

Powell, Walter Clement. "Journal of W. C. Powell." Ed. Charles Kelly. *Utah Historical Quarterly* 16-17 (1948-49): 257-478.

Powell, William S. *The North Carolina Gazetteer.* University of North Carolina Press, Chapel Hill, 1968.

Powell Survey Correspondence.

Official Correspondence of the Geographical and Geological Survey of the Rocky Mountain Region, J. W. Powell in Charge. Record Group 57, U.S. National Archives and Records Service, Washington, 1871-79.

Preuss, Charles. *Exploring with Fremont: The Private Diaries of Charles Preuss, Cartographer for John C. Fremont on his First, Second and Fourth Expeditions.* Trans. and ed. E. G. and E. S. Gudde. University of Oklahoma Press, Norman, 1958.

Pyne, Stephen J. *Grove Karl Gilbert: A Great Engine of Research.* University of Texas Press, Austin, 1980.

Rinhart, Floyd, and Marion Rinhart. *The American Daguerreotype.* University of Georgia Press, Athens, 1981.

Rudisill, Richard. *Mirror Image: The Influence of the Daguerreotype on American Society.* University of New Mexico Press, Albuquerque, 1971.

Rydell, Robert W. "All the World's a Fair: America's International Exhibitions, 1876-1916." Ph.D dissertation, University of California, Los Angeles, 1980.

Scherer, Joanna C. *Indians: The Great Photographs That Reveal North American Indian Life, 1847-1929, from the Unique Collection of the Smithsonian Institution.* Crown Publishers, New York, 1973.

Schroeder, Albert H. "History of Archaeological Research." In Sturtevant, *Handbook of North American Indians* 9: 5-13.

Simpson, James H. *Report of Explorations across the Great Ba-*

sin . . . in 1859. 1876; rpt. University of Nevada Press, Reno, 1983.

Snyder, Joel. *American Frontiers: The Photographs of Timothy O'Sullivan, 1867-1874.* Aperture, Inc., New York, 1981.

Sobieszek, Robert. *Alexander Gardner's Photographs along the 35th Parallel.* George Eastman House, Rochester, N.Y., 1976.

Sondley, F. A. *The Hickory Nut Gorge.* n.p., n.d. Pamphlet on file, North Carolina Department of Cultural Resources, Raleigh, N.C.

Stegner, Wallace. *Beyond the Hundredth Meridian: John Wesley Powell and the Second Opening of the West.* Houghton, Mifflin, Boston, 1962.

Stephens, Hal G., and Eugene M. Shoemaker. *In the Footsteps of John Wesley Powell: An Album of Comparative Photographs of the Green and Colorado Rivers, 1871-72 and 1968.* Johnson Books, Boulder, Colo., 1987.

Stevenson, James. "Illustrated Catalogue of the Collections Obtained from the Indians of New Mexico and Arizona in 1879 [and 1880]." In *Second Annual Report of the Bureau of Ethnology, 1880-1881,* pp. 307-465. Washington, 1883.

Stevenson, Matilda Coxe. "The Sia." In *Eleventh Annual Report of the Bureau of American Ethnology, 1889-1890,* pp. 3-157. Washington, 1894.

———. "The Zuni Indians: Their Mythology, Esoteric Fraternities and Ceremonies." In *Twenty-third Annual Report of the Bureau of American Ethnology, 1901-1902,* pp. 3-634. Washington, 1904.

Steward, Julian H. *Notes on Hillers' Photographs of the Paiute and Ute Indians Taken on the Powell Expedition of 1873.* Smithsonian Miscellaneous Collections, vol. 98, no. 18. Washington, 1939.

Sturhahn, Joan. *Carvalho: Artist-Photographer-Adventurer-Patriot. Portrait of a Forgotten American.* Richwood Pub. Co., Merrick, N.Y., 1976.

Sturtevant, William C., gen. ed. *Handbook of North American Indians.* 20 vols. Smithsonian Institution, Washington, 1976 et seq.

Taft, Robert. *Photography and the American Scene: A Social History, 1839-1889.* Macmillan Co., New York, 1938. Rpt. Dover, New York, 1964.

Teller, H. M. "Order to Bureau of Indian Affairs Staff, Jan. 28, 1884." Copy in Smithsonian National Anthropological Archives, Washington.

Thompson, Almon H. "Diary of Almon Harris Thompson, Geographer. Explorations of the Colorado River of the West and Its Tributaries, 1871-1875." Ed. Herbert E. Gregory. *Utah Historical Quarterly* 7 (1939): 1-140.

Thrapp, Dan L. *The Conquest of Apacheria.* University of Oklahoma Press, Norman, 1967.

Trenholm, Virginia C. *The Arapahoes, Our People.* University of Oklahoma Press, Norman, 1970.

Trennert, Robert A., Jr. "A Grand Failure: The Centennial Indian Exhibition of 1876." *Prologue: The Journal of the National Archives* 6, no. 2 (1974): 118-29.

United States Statutes. *Civil Sundry Appropriation for 1879-1880,* Section XX, 397, 1879.

Viola, Herman J. *Diplomats in Buckskins.* Smithsonian Institution Press, Washington, 1981.

———. *The Indian Legacy of Charles Bird King.* Smithsonian Institution Press, Washington, 1976.

Walcott, Charles D. "Report of the Director." *U.S. Geological Survey, Sixteenth Annual Report,* pp. 7-130. Washington, 1896.

———. "Report of the Director." *U.S. Geological Survey, Seventeenth Annual Report,* pp. 7-200. Washington, 1897.

———. "Report of the Director." *U.S. Geological Survey, Nineteenth Annual Report,* pp. 9-143. Washington, 1899.

———. "Report of the Director." *U.S. Geological Survey, Twentieth Annual Report,* pp. 11-209. Washington, 1900.

Wallace, Edward S. *The Great Reconnaissance: Soldiers, Artists and Scientists on the Frontier, 1848-1861.* Little, Brown, Boston, 1955.

Weitzman, David. *Traces of the Past: A Field Guide to Industrial Archaeology.* Charles Scribner's Sons, New York, 1980.

Welling, William. *Photography in America: The Formative Years, 1839-1900.* Crowell Publishers, New York, 1978.

Weltfish, Gene. *The Lost Universe: The Way of Life of the Pawnee.* Basic Books, New York, 1965.

Wheeler, George M. *Photographs Showing Landscapes, Geological and Other Features of Portions of the Western Territories of the United States, Obtained in Connection with Geographical and Geological Explorations West of the 100th Meridian, Seasons of 1871, 1872, and 1873.* U.S. Army Corps of Engineers, Washington, 1875. Rpt. as *Wheeler's Photographic Survey of the American West, 1871-1873.* Dover, New York, 1983.

Wilkins, Thurman. *Clarence King, a Biography.* Macmillan, New York, 1958.

———. *Thomas Moran, Artist of the Mountains.* University of Oklahoma Press, Norman, 1966.

Wilmerding, John. "The Luminist Movement: Some Reflections." In John Wilmerding, ed., *American Light: The Luminist Movement, 1850-1875. Paintings, Drawings, Photographs.* Harper and Row, New York, and National Gallery of Art, Washington, 1982.

Woodbury, Richard B. "Zuni Prehistory and History to 1850." In Sturtevant, *Handbook of North American Indians* 9: 467-73.

Woodward, Grace S. *The Cherokees.* University of Oklahoma Press, Norman, 1963.

Wright, Muriel H. *A Guide to the Indian Tribes of Oklahoma.* University of Oklahoma Press, Norman, 1951.

This book was produced by the Smithsonian Institution Press
Printed by Kingsport Press, Tennessee
Halftones and duotones by York Graphics, Pennsylvania
Set in Galliard by The TypeWorks, Baltimore, Maryland
Edited by Matthew Abbate
Production coordinated by Kathleen Brown
Designed by Alan Carter